Colonel Parke of Virginia

Daniel Parke of Virginia (1664/5–1710). Painted in London shortly
after the Battle of Blenheim, by John Closterman (1656–1715).
—*Virginia Historical Society*

∴

Colonel Parke of Virginia

"The Greatest Hector in the Town"

a Biography by

Helen Hill Miller

Algonquin Books of Chapel Hill • *1989*

Published by
Algonquin Books of Chapel Hill
Post Office Box 2225
Chapel Hill, North Carolina 27515-2225

a division of
Workman Publishing Company, Inc.
708 Broadway
New York, New York 10003

LIBRARY OF CONGRESS CATALOGING-IN-PUBLICATION DATA
Miller, Helen Hill, 1899–
Colonel Parke of Virginia : the greatest hector in the town : a
biography / by Helen Hill Miller.
p. cm.
Includes bibliographical references.
ISBN 0-912697-87-3
1. Parke, Daniel, 1664/5–1710. 2. Politicians—Virginia—
Biography 3. Virginia—History—Colonial period, ca. 1600—1775.
4. Parke family. 5. Spanish Succession, War of, 1701–1714—
Campaigns. 6. Colonial administrators—Great Britain—Biography.
I. Title.
F229.0P27M55 1989
975.5'02'092—dc20
[B] 89-17640
CIP

First Edition
1 3 5 7 9 10 8 6 4 2

To Pickens Miller,

Who Identified the Medal Shown Beside Parke

In the Closterman Portrait (see Frontispiece).

This Was the Medal Voted to Parke

by the Dutch States General

for Bringing the News Of the Victory at Blenheim.

Contents

Illustrations

Note on Sources

ADEQUATE acknowledgment of the kindness and help that I received while working on this book is impossible. It goes without saying that my mistakes are my own. They are the less excusable in view of all the aid I received from those who guided me among the original documents of four widely separated geographic areas—Virginia, England, Bavaria, and the Leeward Islands of the Caribbean.

The range of available data can be illustrated: in Virginia, the day-to-day minutes of the Governor-in-Council and the House of Burgesses, the York County Court, and Bruton Parish vestry include specific information about government events while the Parkes were members of these institutions.

Comparable surviving records detail the life of the Evelyn branch of the family on both sides of the Atlantic. The colonial story is told in the family records as well as in early histories. The diary of John Evelyn combines private events and a broad coverage of public affairs in the mother country and on the Continent. And the Evelyn letters in the library of Christ Church College, Oxford, describe the effort made on behalf of young Daniel Parke by his English kinsfolk. For the period of Parke's London quest for the Virginia governorship, the *House of Commons Journals* chronicle the extent of bribery and corruption in the borough of Malmesbury (Wiltshire), where he suffered his defeat for a seat in Parliament.

The manuscript collection of the British Library contains correspondence essential to the tracing of Parke's activities. The Public Record Office preserves his correspondence with various secretaries of state and the Lords of Trade and Plantations during his tenure as governor of the Leeward Islands. Official accounts of his murder and privately published pamphlets display the usual contradictions among eyewitnesses of unexpected violence. And the court cases arising under his will record the controversy he continued to stir for close to half a century after his death.

On-site visits to places of historical events connected with their subjects are the duty of all biographers, and in this case provided deeper insight into the subject, as I found during my inspection of the Schellenberg hill on the Danube. Here, control of the entire countryside depended on control of the fort at the top. Most documentation of the Allied troops' agony as they climbed from river level to that fort, under bombardment from the town of Donau-wörth, gained a little each time the tale was told. In the memory of survivors, the hillside, whose steep sides they had pulled themselves up by grasping slippery grasses, became a mountain.

Historical specialists, archivists, librarians and their staffs in England, Washington, and Virginia put me in touch with manuscripts, government records, personal correspondence, maps and prints, and portraits. I am especially grateful for the assistance, over a long time, of the staffs of the Folger Shakespeare Library in Washington, D.C., especially Nati Krivatsy; the Virginia Historical Society in Richmond, especially Virginius Hall; the Colonial Williamsburg Foundation; and the Lloyd House Collection of Virginiana at the Public Library of Alexandria, Virginia. In England I was assisted by experts at the Manuscript Collection of the British Library, the Print Room of the British Museum, Christ Church College Library at Oxford, and a sequence of military historians at Sandhurst and a number of universities.

It was Gale Pierce who bravely put the resulting manuscript into her computer, and when it came out it was read by three people in whom my debt culminates. As an editor, Louis Rubin can convert reported research into literary writing in a single phrase; as a critic, he can deal with trouble from afar. From his own writing, Parke Rouse knows seventeenth- and early eighteenth-century Virginia as few others do; he can spot an author's misplacement, even of an FFV's far-removed cousin, before injury occurs. Thad Tate, Director of Williamsburg's Institute of Early American History and

Culture and editor of the *William and Mary Quarterly*, approaches a manuscript with his long experience of dealing with many such efforts; nevertheless, he points out what is missing, and amiss, with a twinkle in his eye.

To all who worked with me, and over me, I extend my appreciative thanks.

Helen Hill Miller

Foreword

DANIEL Parke, Jr., never lacked for a ready answer. By the time this infant, born on a colonial plantation in York County, Virginia, in the mid-1660s, was old enough to respond to a visiting gentleman's foreseeable question, "What do you want to do when you grow up?" he solemnly announced a purpose that he cherished to the last day of his life: "I would like to be Governor of Virginia, Sir."

And by governor he did not mean one of the deputies who came to the colony and managed it under the direction of the Lords of Trade and Plantations in London, even though that man was addressed in Virginia as "Governor." He meant the man to whom the English sovereign awarded the title and who, more often than not, sent someone else to do the day-to-day governing while he continued his life in London at the center of English affairs, as a courtier and companion of other Restoration rakes who clustered around the Stuart kings.

For better or for worse, and by curious coincidence, in the course of his life Parke was an actor in three of the geographic areas where the seventeenth-century history of the Western world took a decisive turn: during the development of England's first permanent colony in America; in the decisive test of strength at Blenheim between the combined armies of France and Bavaria and the forces assembled by John Churchill, duke of Marlborough, from England, Holland, and Germany; and on the frontier of the eastern Caribbean islands that opened to conquest as the Spanish presence in America waned.

Precociously, well before he came of age, young Parke was making calculated moves toward his coveted preferment. After education in England he returned to Virginia and contracted a politically useful marriage. In 1679 his father's death left him a wealthy man and York County's largest landowner, with a home plantation a few miles from the settlement that, by the end of the century, had succeeded Jamestown as the capital of Virginia. In the mid-1690s, from election to election and appointment to appointment, he quickly worked his way up in the colony's public service until he occupied a seat on the Governor's Council, with emoluments that included a well-paid collectorship of the revenue and the colonelcy of the county militia. For two years he basked in these additions to his estate, while every indication promised him a brilliant career.

Yet some of his behavior during this period raised questions about his future. On a visit to England with his uncle Philip Ludwell he had observed the lascivious life of the Court, and on his return to Virginia he brought with him an English mistress, who shortly gave birth to a son. Parke, who saw to it that his child was referred to as his godson, named him Julius Caesar. In 1697 when he moved to England to be on the spot to press for the Virginia governorship, he raised eyebrows by sailing with his mistress and leaving the boy to be brought up by his wife along with their two legitimate daughters. (She was also to manage his plantations.)

During this same interval, Parke engaged in a series of public quarrels involving two governors and the commissary of the Bishop of London. He had become a swaggerer, offering to duel on little or no provocation. Since the Rev. James Blair's clerical gown protected him from a challenge, Parke's attack took the spectacular form of dragging Blair's wife, during divine service, out of the Bruton church pew where she had been sitting at the invitation of the Ludwells. Governor Andros was Parke's hero, and Governor Nicholson, now moved to the government of Maryland, his favorite target.

On reaching England he decided to seek recognition as a member of the House of Commons: Parliament was coming into increased importance in the governmental structure. It was also a time of exceptional bribery and corruption in the constituencies, especially in the so-called "rotten" boroughs of scandalously limited franchise. When public outcry necessitated a show of virtue in the election of 1701, parliamentary investigation brought in more than a score of constituencies for scrutiny. Malmesbury (in Wiltshire) was one of them, and it was there that Parke stood. He had participated in the usual practices, offering money where it could prove useful. Two more experienced hands were returned as the borough's members, and Parke's misdoings were chronicled in the *Journals of the House of Commons.*

If civilian distinction was not to be his, he could seek military glory. The War of the Spanish Succession was beginning; Parke went to the Netherlands and offered himself as a volunteer under Lord Marlborough. By the time of the Blenheim campaign in 1704 he had maneuvered himself into a position as one of the aides-de-camp attached to Marlborough's staff at general headquarters.

At the end of the battle of Blenheim he was in attendance on his chief and became the bearer of the news of the Alliance's tremendous victory to Queen Anne. For a brief but glorious interval he regaled the English capital, the only person in London to have been present at the encounter. He commissioned a number of artists to paint his portrait and had no doubt that the coveted governorship of Virginia would shortly be his.

He was wrong. When honors were distributed, the negotiations that achieved the union of England and Scotland in 1707 were already under way; one of Marlborough's most effective generals, the Scottish lord, George Hamilton, earl of Orkney, was given the post, which not only recognized past performance but assured enthusiasm for union among the tobacco merchants in Glasgow.

Instead of the post he wanted, Parke was named governor of an English-held group of small islands in the West Indies, the Leewards, part of the Lesser Antilles chain. He postponed his departure as long as possible, and, disappointed and recalcitrant, he served unworthily when he arrived. The award-makers were primarily interested in governors who could command English troops and draw the colonies that had been founded with different purposes and at various times into a unified imperial system. Economic affairs were treated as secondary; although one of a governor's main functions was to suppress smuggling, everyone smuggled.

In a short time, ranking settlers on the islands began to file written complaints of Parke's public behavior with the Lords of Trade and Plantations; they took increasing umbrage at the loose morals of his private life. By the end of 1710 affairs had reached a crisis, and a riot at Government House on the island of Antigua terminated in his murder.

At that very moment in England, right-wing High Tories were satisfying a long political jealousy by ousting Marlborough and Godolphin from their control of public affairs. Far away on a colonial island, the sitting governor might be slaughtered by those Whitehall had appointed him to govern, but the event was a dark spot on the far horizon, while at home at the palace the famous Sarah, Duchess of Marlborough, was fighting a losing battle against displacement as the confidante of Queen Anne. Parke was a Marlborough appointee, and Her Majesty shortly bestowed a pardon on the rioters. His ignominious death in the Caribbean thus ended a life that had begun with the ambition to be royal governor of Virginia.

There was an aftermath. For half a century after his death, Parke's will, which gave preferential treatment to his illegitimate, as compared with his legitimate offspring, gave him a lively memorial in the courts of Virginia, England, and the Islands. Another kind of permanence resulted from the marriages of his two legitimate daughters, which carried the Parke blood into the mainstream of American history.

What went wrong was in part a matter of character. Parke had all the vices of a Restoration rake. When he and his mistress sailed from Virginia in 1697 never to return, he deserted his wife and children, while continuing to absorb a major part of the annual yield of the plantations managed by his wife. His promised dowries for his daughters were never paid. He had an immense capacity for accumulating debt, borrowing left and right from anyone who would help him sustain his English life-style. He died obligated to two of his sisters, his mistress, his London agent, and a multitude of others whose subsequent claims diminished the financial status of his legitimate heirs. He was a cultivator of anyone who could forward his advance, nimbly shifting attachments in the light of changed circumstances and dominating those he could outweigh.

At the same time, his life exhibited the chief virtue of the Restoration rake, personal courage. In Marlborough's army, he was a volunteer; in 1704 his responsibilities were limited to those of an aide-de-camp. Yet, when all was at stake and nothing was certain, at the opening of the fight to control the fortress atop the Schellenberg, Parke reassembled the fragments of the first unit of the attack, both of whose officers had been killed; he led the remaining men, under cannonfire, into the mêlée that forced the entrance. And at Antigua, when Government House was taken by the rioters, he stood alone, refusing to surrender the commission given him by the Queen. He was a soldier's soldier.

But if Parke's failed career was due in part to his character, it was also a foreseeable result of the English social system. The colonies were not a field to which Whitehall looked for gubernatorial material. From the founding of Jamestown to the American Revolution, no other Virginian was named to the office to which Parke aspired. His mother might be a cousin of John Evelyn, a familiar of the court and the chronicler of the Restoration; but she and his father and his father's father were colonials. Parke had served his apprenticeship in governmental affairs in the offices of his native Virginia, not in Parliament.

His first defeat in England was illustrative. The men who struggled against each other in the 1701 parliamentary election were already powers in Whitehall, fully able to protect themselves and their protégés: the Lords Wharton and Halifax from the London financial community; Samuel Shepherd of the East India Company; Sir Charles Hedges, one of the current secretaries of state; and a popular incumbent seeking reelection. Against their established influence Parke had little chance; through John Evelyn he had the third Lord Peterborough as a sponsor, but Peterborough too was a new player in that part of the county.

When Parke moved to the Continent, he ranked only as an aide-de-camp. He had written his elder daughter that he expected to be given the colonelcy of one of the famous old regiments in English history; but he was not even made a colonel of one of the many new units formed when Parliament raised the numbers of the armed forces from 7,000 to 40,000 at the beginning of the war. So when the rewards of Blenheim were distributed it was hardly surprising that a lieutenant general was named for Virginia, and that Parke was sent to govern a group of small islands in the Caribbean, where the governor was expected to take up residence, as the lieutenant governor did in Williamsburg.

Prior to the end of the seventeenth century, when a new English arrival put in an appearance in Virginia he was welcomed by similar English gentlemen already in residence. A hierarchy was in formation, but the availability of free land and the relatively small numbers of high-ranking citizens tempered the competition that developed later. By contrast, a Virginia gentleman returning to England, unless he was coming back to retire, had to learn that the path to preferment was far more heavily traveled in a mature society where orderly sequences regulated the advancement of talent, and where, in Parke's case, they did so to his exclusion.

Colonel Parke of Virginia

Chapter 1

Origins

AGAINST the backdrop of history, movements of individuals take on antlike proportions. Yet the cumulative effect of those tiny, moving dots shapes that history, and during the first third of the seventeenth century lines of emigration from Europe suddenly extended themselves to settle colonies in the soil of the New World.

In the high councils of the countries from which they came, the directors of policy were interpreting, for their respective nations, the meaning of the preceding Age of Discovery. After a millennium-long confinement to the European continent and the Mediterranean coast of Africa, these directors now had before them a round globe of enticing scope, instead of their customary flat map.

With the failure of the Armada in 1588, Spain had lost a crucial contest with England, and English settlers were taking ship for new ventures on the northern continent of the new West. At the same time, armed forces from Holland and France, as well as England, were landing on the barrier of Caribbean islands that had formerly protected Spain's American empire. In the opposite direction from Europe and half a world away, English, Dutch, and French enterprises were competing for control of trade with the East Indies and the Orient. Strategies were changing: recent events had revealed to the English the possibility of world rule through sea power.

Simultaneous movements were changing the shape of more familiar places in Europe. Louis XIV of France was expanding a land empire whose dimensions threatened to minimize the presence of other long-recognized powers. Spreading his European control both north and south, he had already replaced the Spanish as occupiers of the Dutch provinces across from England along the North Sea and was preparing to make his own grandson heir to Spain's monarchy.

To both the English and the northern Europeans, the French advance carried a religious threat: they were the remaining exponents of the Protestant Reformation, while France, since revocation of the Edict of Nantes, had become militantly Catholic. Within England, a domestic conflict with Protestant roots ranged Puritans against Royalists in a challenge to the absolutist doctrine of kingly rule by divine right—a doctrine vigorously adhered to by Louis of France as well as the Stuart dynasty. For an interval in midcentury, after the Cromwellian revolution had executed Charles I, England had been a parliamentary republic; and within three decades after the Stuarts were restored to the throne, the Glorious Revolution authorized the establishment by Parliament of a new form of government: a Protestant constitutional monarchy limited by the Bill of Rights.

This book follows the fortunes of one of the individuals whose parents were among the multitude in the antlike procession that reached North America in the first years of settlement. At midcentury, two English families of the upper gentry were joined in Virginia when the elder Daniel Parke, son of a family of Essex origin who had become moderately successful London merchants, married a widow, born Rebecca Evelyn, daughter of a Surrey family engaged since Queen Elizabeth's time in the enjoyment of a monopoly for the manufacture of gunpowder.

Both had been preceded to the New World by earlier generations. When the will of William Parke of London, drawn on November 13, 1633, was probated the following year, note was taken that he had died "beyond seas." Daniel Parke, his youngest son, who apparently stayed in London longer than the other members of his family, received £100. Among other directions to the executor, William Parke's elder son William, was the stipulation of a pay-

"A Map of Virginia Discovered to the Hills." From the *Blathwayt Atlas*, showing English holdings on the American East Coast from Cape Cod to Cape Fear.—*John Work Garrett Library, Johns Hopkins University*

ment to "Adam Thorowgood of Virginia, Gent. 50 shillings worth of commodities."* Years later, a patent carried not only the younger William's name but that of his father and his mother Sarah (to whom the will had left £150). William also witnessed a York County, Virginia, deed for his brother Daniel in 1652, the year when Daniel's name first appears in Virginia records.

By the 1650s two courses were open to newcomers to the colony.

---

*The Adam Thoroughgood house in Norfolk is one of the very earliest brick houses in the Old Dominion.

Particularly if a settler brought some capital to invest, he was apt to secure a plantation on the lower portion of the Virginia peninsula that lies between the James and the York rivers and terminates at Hampton Roads, where the Chesapeake Bay flows out into the Atlantic.

The colony's capital was established at Jamestown, on the south shore of the peninsula. In 1662, the Assembly passed an act for the building of a town there, stipulating that thirty-two houses should be put up, each with ground-floor dimensions of forty by twenty feet. They were to be two and a half stories high, of brick with slate or tile roofs. They were not to be scattered, but "regularly placed one by another or in some such forme as the honorable Sir William Berkeley shall appoint."[1]

Excavations, begun in 1912, located a 280-foot line of foundations believed to be those of this first group. Part of one of the houses, built by William Sherwood, was rented to serve as the "Country House," the official headquarters of the governor and the place where the Governor's Council and the House of Burgesses met.[2] On April 10, 1665, the colony's secretary, Thomas Ludwell, reported to London that the town was "capable (at present) for ye Civill Administracon, & an introduction to a ffactorie for producing silk, flax, potashes & English-grains."

But the site that became Jamestown had not been wisely chosen. The first settlers had faced anxiously east, hopeful of English sails on the horizon bringing supplies and more settlers, and fearful of discovery by Spanish galleons determined to hold the New World for their own. But by the latter years of the century, most settlers had turned their sights westward, pushing the Indians before them as they sought their fortunes not from the water but from the land. Their town had been well placed either to avoid or to ward off Spanish attack; it was close to the entry of the James River into Chesapeake Bay, and hidden from the gap between the two capes named for James I's elder sons, where the Bay flows out into the Atlantic Ocean. Unclogged by shoals, the waters were ample for the maneuver of deep-draft sailing ships in the event of war. Yet it was not suitable for ordinary living.

For swampy land was unhealthy land, and on Jamestown's landward side, swamps were everywhere. During Bacon's Rebellion in 1676, the frontier settlers lost their young leader to fever caught when he and his troops lay in fetid water that made an island of the capital. And the residents of the capital paid a similar price, summer after summer, in deaths from malaria.

Jamestown was also frequently damaged by fire. When the third state house burned just as the town was recovering from the flames of the rebellion, serious consideration of an alternative site turned to a hamlet a few miles northwest of Jamestown in York County. Called Middle Plantation, it had been laid off on higher ground in 1632. This was the future Williamsburg.

In the early years, the site had been close to the limit of organized English occupation: just beyond it, a six-mile-long palisade, built as a barrier to Indian incursions, crossed the peninsula from one river to the other; stout bars could be slipped across inside the gates at night. Life below the palisade symbolized permanence. Life above it, where counties had been laid off, but where the few inhabitants were largely on their own, merged imperceptibly with the western wilderness. Settlers who located there, with little beside their bare hands as capital, were genuine frontiersmen.

The Parkes were people of the protected area. The senior Daniel Parke's first land purchases were prudently selected with the eye of an experienced merchant. They lay just ahead of advancing settlement and were sure to rise in value as more newcomers appeared. Middle Plantation was served by two creeks, one flowing south to the shore of the James, the other flowing north to the shore of the York River; both permitted transport of goods far more easily than by road.

Daniel Parke I set up his home plantation of some 300 acres near the upper end of Queen's Creek where it joined the York nearly opposite Gloucester Point. The location placed him within ten miles of Middle Plantation and not more than twice that distance from Jamestown. Gradually he acquired a considerable portion of the land to which Middle Plantation expanded, and in the course of time he became the largest landowner in York County. Today no vestige of his Queen's Creek house remains, nor of the mill that he operated in the area.

Supplementing these primary acquisitions, he then bought land further west. His total properties eventually numbered in the neighborhood of 10,000 acres: when his executors visited the cultivated plantations, they stopped at Parke Hall, Parke Level, Parke Manor, and Parke Meadow in addition to Queen's Creek. On the strength of these holdings he—and his son after him—were recognized as ranking citizens.

Meanwhile, on the Evelyn side of the family, most of the sons of George, the first monopolist, continued to make gunpowder at various locations in Surrey. Among them, however, the first Robert Evelyn proved no businessman. He inherited from his father a property at Godstone on the Surrey-Kent border and married Susanna, daughter of Gregory Young, a London grocer. He then sank so far into debt as to be twice imprisoned. For him, emigration was an escape: he sold his inheritance to his brother John, paid off what he could, and departed after writing a lament of farewell to his stepmother:

> I am very sorry that I am mortgaged so much, that I am driven to tell you to pay the hundred marks to Mr. Stoughton for me, which you at my request did stand bound so kindly for me to him. . . . I am going to the sea, a long and dangerous vo[yage with] other men, to make me to be [able] to pay my debts . . . and I beseech you, if I do die, that you would be good unto my poor wife and children, which, God knows, I shall leave very poor.[3]

This Robert never returned. Twenty-odd years later, a new generation of Evelyns, two of them again named George and Robert, were brought to Virginia by the first Robert's brother-in-law, their uncle Thomas Young. He landed on July 3, 1634, bearing a pass from Charles I enjoining the Virginians to aid them in every particular.

Young also had authorization to explore the area between Virginia and New England. Using this, he took his nephews, along with other passengers from his ship, north to the Delaware River and built a fort at Eriwomeck, intending to open trade with the Indians. When slow delivery of trading goods disappointed them, they turned south into Virginia and joined Virginia Councilman William Claiborne at a similar outpost previously set up by him on Kent Island in Chesapeake Bay.

This island was disputed territory: the charter granted by Charles I to the Lords Baltimore in 1632 transferred to the jurisdiction of their new colony of Maryland all waters east of the south bank of the Potomac where it empties into the Bay and all uninhabited islands surrounded by those waters. Irate that Maryland had refused to recognize Claiborne's prior occupancy, and generally grieved by a grant that carved the colony of Maryland out of the northeast corner of what Virginians had previously taken to be Virginia, some citizens of the Virginia colony joined Claiborne in offering vigorous resistance.

The Evelyns were at the center of the disturbance. Robert's brother George became the agent of the Clonberry Company of London, with whom Claiborne had a contract for trade goods. Here too deliveries were very slow in arriving; when the first ship finally came in, George took it to Jamestown on a trip to seek support from the Virginia governor. Since the governor was under royal instruction to help the Baltimores, George got no help. He thereupon sold the ship and the goods, returned to Kent Island, changed sides in the controversy, and joined forces with Maryland's Governor Leonard Calvert. Calvert named him commandant of Kent and lord of a manor to be called Evelinton. A month later, Calvert's troops forced the Kent Islanders to surrender and accept the island's inclusion in Maryland's territory. George continued as commandant until 1638.

Both of the brothers had bought land in James City County, Virginia, soon after arrival, but neither of them made a fortune in the New World, though over the years they acquired a certain amount of standing. In 1637 Robert was appointed Virginia's surveyor of lands and was named to the Governor's Council. He also served in the Maryland Assembly of 1637–1638. Both men maintained their interest in Captain Young's first settlement on the Delaware, now incorporated into the County Palatine of New Albion. When another Englishman, Beauchamp Plantagenet, published a prospectus for this province in 1648, he included a long letter from George describing and extolling the merits of the place and offering to advise settlers preparing to go there.

Like his predecessor, Robert is believed to have remained in the New World permanently and to have died in the West Indies. George, who had earned the nickname "Captain George" by several voyages to and from England in the 1640s, returned home to stay; by 1649 he was engaged in a building project for his uncle at Wotton in Surrey.

But George left descendants in the colony, for on one of his voyages he brought to Virginia two of his children, a boy and a girl. (George and his wife had separated before his initial departure; these two children had been cared for by Lady Bodley, daughter of Thomas Evelyn of Long Ditton.) His son Mountjoy was put to learning the Indian trade with the king of the Powtomacks; he married a daughter of the Robins family in Northumberland County on Virginia's Eastern Shore and purchased 600 acres of land in James City County in 1651.

George's daughter Rebecca married one Bartholomew Knipe, gentleman, purchaser in 1652 of a 418-acre tract in James City County,[4] and became the mother of a son, Christopher. Like many others, however, she was widowed before long, and by the second half of the 1650s she had married again. Her "now husband," as the phrase ran, was the thriving London immigrant, Daniel Parke of Queen's Creek.

Three of the Parkes' first living children were girls: Evelyn, Rebecca, and Jane. Like most other couples of the time, they also had babies who died at or near birth. The Bruton parish register shows one little boy, Feilding, who died in July 1662, and another, Daniel, who died in October 1663. When the next baby, presumably in 1664–1665, proved also to be a boy, the parents followed a custom common in both England and America: they gave the new arrival the name they had chosen for his immediate predecessor. This Daniel lived, and was the child who wanted to be governor.

Chapter 2

Parke's English Cousinry

In 1671, at just the time when young Daniel Parke reached the age for serious education, Virginia's governor, Sir William Berkeley, in the acerbic tone he used during his second administration, assured the Lords of Trade of his thankfulness that in Virginia "there are no free schools or printing and I hope we shall not have, these hundred years."

Though girls were generally taught to read and write, nobody was unduly concerned about the lack of further schooling for the daughters. The scion of a well-known family, however, required the polish of a gentleman, and in Virginia private tutors were scarce and sometimes of doubtful quality. So when her son was ready, Rebecca Parke packed up her children and returned to live in the midst of her Evelyn relatives at Long Ditton, Surrey, where a suitable school or tutor would be available for him.

In England, good local schools were still exceptional, though the town of Guildford, only a few miles from Long Ditton, had had a fine grammar school since Tudor times, and the gunpowder magnate had placed one of his sons there. (While the early records of this school no longer exist, a reference in John Evelyn's *Diary* confirms this boy's attendance.) The diarist himself had been intended for Eton, the great public school instituted by King Henry VI in 1440 and located nearby on the Thames, just across Windsor Bridge; but the boy's insistence—to his adult regret—on remaining with his maternal grandparents at Lewes put him instead in the Free School at Southoven. Fortunately, in England first-rate tutors were glad to attach themselves to a family of the gentry, for such a position could well lead to a career as a don in one of the Oxford or Cambridge colleges. In the case of the Evelyns' former tutor, Mr. Bohun, it did so.

Tutors were expected to impart a curriculum that included Latin and quite possibly Greek; a combination of history, philosophy, and literature derived from the great books of the classical period; and mathematics. In addition, their charges were expected to become familiar with the art and architecture to be seen on the Grand Tour, on which, quite often, the family tutor acted as guide and mentor.

Over the next years young Daniel received the preparation of a gentleman, and at the same time he came to know the children and the uncles and the aunts of his mother's ramified cousinry.

The village of Long Ditton, where Parke's mother had grown up and to which she now returned, was where the family founder, the George Evelyn of 1526–1603, had begun his purchases of real estate on the strength of his new prosperity. It lay south of his former residence at Kingston. In the 1560s he bought two of the four manor houses in the Long Ditton vicinity: his eldest grandson, Sir Thomas Evelyn, later occupied the one whose grounds were immediately adjacent to the church. A third manor house came into the family when it was inherited by Dame Anne, Sir Thomas's wife; the fourth dwindled to the status of a farmhouse. So until the last years of the century, when the male line of this branch of the family died out, the Evelyns lived in the village and set the tone of village affairs. During the Cromwellian interregnum, there were occasions when that tone was loudly vociferous.

Rebecca Parke had doubtless recounted to her Virginia family the story of the quarrel between the squire and the rector that temporarily closed the church in the 1650s. Sir Thomas, although a member of Parliament, was by no means a Parliamentarian in the sense of being a Cromwell supporter. He was a high church royalist and was repelled by the Puritan sympathies of the Rev. Richard Byfield, who had become rector in 1629.

In 1634, the High Church Archbishop William Laud required all clergy to read to their congregations from the recently issued *Book of Sports*, which declared the church's (and Crown's) attitude on Sunday behavior. In sharp contrast to the Puritan view that stipulated reflection, prayer, church-going, and the reading of scripture as the only suitable Sunday occupations, this book gave official sanction to Sunday afternoon enjoyment of Morris dancing, bowling on the green, and other similar forms of public diversion. The Rev. Mr. Byfield, by refusing to read the book aloud, brought on himself a three-year suspension from his pulpit.

But the Rev. Richard Hinde, who occupied Mr. Byfield's place during his absence, held similar views; and so one Sunday, in the church sanctuary, an open—and loud—quarrel broke out between him and Dame Anne Evelyn. The exchange continued outdoors across the churchyard until the gate to the manor house grounds closed behind her. The incident was reviewed by higher authority, and the bishop insisted on the rendering of a most reluctant apology.

As soon as the Rev. Mr. Byfield was restored, he and Sir Thomas fell out over plans for much-needed repairs to the church: the roof had developed serious leaks. A sum of £100, earmarked for such use, was in Sir Thomas's hands, but he refused to release it because he heartily disapproved of the rector's intention to rebuild the interior of the edifice as a single large meeting room, free of what Byfield termed the superstitious division of the building into chancel, nave, and porch. When Mr. Byfield appealed to the Lord Protector, Oliver Cromwell himself came to Long Ditton and thought he had settled the parish differences. In departing, he even made a contribution of £100 of his own to be added to the fund.

But he reckoned without the determination of Sir Thomas, who held off repairs until the church became so leaky that services had to be held elsewhere. Not until the 1670s, well after the Stuart Restoration, was the building restored to the conventional form displayed

St. Mary's Church, Long Ditton. Engraving, made about 1720, of the church attended by the senior branch of the Evelyns when Rebecca Evelyn Parke returned to England for her son's education.—*The Rector and Church-wardens of St. Mary's Church, Long Ditton, Surrey*

Wotton House, Surrey. The north front, from the frontispiece of Gideon D. Scull's *The Evelyns in America*, printed for private circulation by Parker & Co., Oxford, 1881.—*Virginia Historical Society*

in an engraving of about 1720.* (Later in the eighteenth century, an all-new church, the present edifice, was erected at another site in the churchyard. A special garden, in which sunken stones indicate the outlines of earlier sanctuaries, permits parishioners to use the spot where the earlier churches stood as a place of rest and reflection.)[1]

By the time Rebecca Parke returned home, Sir Thomas's son, Sir Edward, had succeeded him at the manor. The funeral monument of Edward's daughter Penelope attracted the attention of the antiquary John Aubrey, whose travels around England coincided with the years of Parke's stay. In his *Natural History and Antiquities of the County of Surrey* he says of St. Mary's, Long Ditton, that it is "a handsome church, comprised of a Body and two Isles." He calls attention, among its "Remarkables," to an inscription that credits this Penelope, who died at forty-two, with bearing seventeen children in twenty-four years.[2]

Further south in Surrey, and at Godstone on the eastern border with Kent, the family founder bought additional estates for his three younger sons, thus fostering a burgeoning Evelyn population. The Evelyn showplace, where the founder had lived during his final years, was the manor house at Wotton, southwest of Dorking and six miles from Guildford.

In this lovely rolling country between the North and the South Downs, Leigh Mountain is the tallest prominence on England's south coast. It rises only 965 feet above sea level, but from its top on a bright, clear day the Channel, some thirty miles away, can be seen, twinkling its waters beyond field after lush field of green pasture. The Wotton manor house lies about halfway up this height in a little valley; the property was held by the Evelyn family for over four hundred years until, in the 1980s, it was sold to undergo massive commercial restoration of its formerly superb gardens and varied interior. Its period brick walls witness the arrangements and

---

*Peter Fussell, church warden at Long Ditton, most graciously gave me much information about the mid-seventeenth century community and the Evelyns there, and contributed the sketch of the church as it appeared after restoration.

additions of intervening generations, from the huge Tudor chimneys of the original structure to the diamond-patterned exterior walls of a nineteenth-century renovation. Within, there is a wealth of over-mantels, painted ceilings, and decorative plaster work.

By Daniel Parke's boyhood, ownership of Wotton House had de-scended from the founder's son Richard to Rebecca Parke's cousin, Richard's son George. Here there was much to delight youngsters. They could share their elders' less-than-normally-formal teas in the two-story garden folly known as the Tortoise House—a brick-walled structure with the fourth side left open, its roof supported by columns with massive Tuscan capitals. The open side faced a large sunken tank in which watchers from the second floor of the folly could overlook shadowy black turtles paddling about below the sur-face or laboriously hauling their heavy bodies out onto floating logs to sun themselves: the sharp-clawed ends of their footpads scratchily sought purchase as each tipped the weight of its unwieldy carapace out of the water.

Another inviting site for young adventure was the grotto on the opposite side of the garden, an eerie circular cave cut out of black earth, the strata of its central pillar so sharply outlined as to give the appearance of carved stone. To run off excess energy, cousins could race breathless to the top of the high mound at the right of the garden, which was terraced in its upper reaches and topped by a summer house with a superb view of fields that breathed bucolic well-being. On this expedition, great care had to be taken not to trample the carefully collected specimens of unusual flowers and shrubs. Uncle George would have no patience with that.

For the children, the family's weekly church-going at Wotton held special attraction. St. John's church stands alone in a little val-ley a few miles away.[3] Legend has it that many centuries before, after invading Danes had sacked the area on a raid that took them as far north as Dorking, the Wotton village that then surrounded the church was never restored. St. John's Evelyn Chapel, derived from a former lady chapel, contained—and contains—family funeral monuments illustrating the Evelyn descent from generation to generation.

The founder's monument offered special inducement to count and recount. On the upper level of the columned black marble structure, a kneeling figure of the Elizabethan George looks directly at the beholder. To his right and left, at the ends of the next level, kneel his two wives, facing toward him, and so toward each other. They were the Lady Rose, who died in 1577 after bearing sixteen children, and Lady Joan, whom he married the next year, and who gave birth to another eight children before his death in 1603. But the children's interest was far less in these grownups than in the figures on the tomb's lowest level, a border running across the entire width of the monument. There, effigies display the parents' entire brood, all sixteen boys and eight girls born during the founder's lifetime. The babies who died soon after birth are shown in their swaddling clothes lying in their bassinets. The boys and girls who grew up, but died before their father did, appear with skulls over their heads. Those who lived to be heirs are shown in full figure. All are robed in white.

After an awed interval of observation, what child could resist asking questions:

How many of the children can you name?
Which wife was my great-great-grandmother?
Why did the babies die?
Which of the boys and girls who grew up can you remember?
Where are their families now? (Young Parke could add new American material to previous answers to this question.)

No matter how often repeated, a visit to the family chapel made Sunday at Wotton a banner day.

For all of these descendants, Wotton House remained a kind of family center. Evelyns other than the current proprietor often took a hand in its appearance, among them Captain George. As soon as he returned from America in the 1640s he undertook a number of commissions as a builder. Henry Howard, future Duke of Norfolk, also held a number of properties in Surrey, and Evelyn sons had been educated along with young Howards at the family's castle at Arundel. When the diarist John Evelyn was on his Grand Tour, the current Henry Howard and he had been companions in Venice. One of Captain George's early commissions was to build a great banqueting house for Howard at his Surrey residence at Albury. Soon after completing it, George constructed an elaborate Palladian portico for the Wotton garden. This was a spacious affair: in the center a statue of Venus held a dolphin from whose mouth water flowed into a central pool; at each end, boys' heads spouted water into two smaller stone basins. The floor was paved with marble and the painted ceiling displayed the four elements, the goddess Flora, and the family arms. Captain George's cousin John, who from 1643 to the end of his long life was also designing and redesigning the Wotton garden, was critical of this structure: his diary for February 26, 1649, comments: "Came to see me Capt. *Geo. Evelyn* my kindsman the greate Travellor, & one who believed himselfe a better *Architect* than realy he was, witnesse the *Portico* in the *Garden* at *Wotton*; yet the greate room at *Alburie* is somewhat better understood: he had a large mind, but overbuilt every thing."[4]

In 1653, the proprietor of Wotton executed some major plans: he built a banqueting hall some eighty-eight feet long, twenty wide and twenty high; and with his brother John's advice, he redesigned his garden with formal walks, terraces, and a fountain, in the Italian style brought over from the Continent with the vogue for Palladian architecture.

Among the galaxy of Evelyn children who were Daniel Parke's companions, one of the John Evelyns became a special friend with whom Daniel kept in touch in later years. A decade older than Daniel, when he was almost twelve he went up to Oxford, "under the inspection of Dr. Ralph Bathhurst, President of Trinity, having first got his Latin and Greek at home under the tutelage of Dr. Ralph Bohun," who by now was a fellow of New College. Five years later, his father, by then having announced "my intention being he should seriously apply himself to a study of law" saw the boy "specially admitted of the Middle Temple, by Sir Fra: North, Her Majesties Solicitor General." (Evelyn could be relied on to know the right man for the occasion.)

This John's father, often referred to as "Sylva" because of a very successful book on the culture of trees and the importance of planting them that he published in 1664, was in many ways an exception to the Evelyn squirearchy. Almost alone among his generation, for many years he did not live in Surrey. As a young man whose Grand Tour was prolonged by the uncertainties of the Cromwellian revolution at home, he had spent some time in Paris, where he met the Stuart ambassadorial representative, Sir Richard Browne and married his only daughter, Mary.

Before going abroad as a diplomat, Sir Richard had owned and lived in Sayes Court, a considerable estate at Deptford on the Thames east of London. This holding had been sequestered by the Puritans, but in 1653 John Evelyn was able to negotiate its return. His young bride joined him, and for the ensuing forty years the couple lived there. Yet their final residence was back in the home county. At the end of the century John's brother George, after the death of his last male offspring left him alone in the great rooms at Wotton, invited them to come and keep him company; and John became his heir.

John Evelyn was a figure in the great world that circled around the Restoration court. All through his life, his daily rounds brought him into intimate contact with more facets of English society than most other members of the Enlightenment era. Like the rest of the family, he had always been a Royalist, and from the 1660s on he was on close terms of friendship with each of the successive Stuart kings. Yet his devotion was more to an abstraction than an actuality: almost as a Puritan might, he abhorred the lascivious life-style of the mistress-ridden monarchy and avoided much of the Court's evening festivity by not living in town. For years he used a pied-à-terre maintained by his father-in-law at St. James's for overnight stays; and in his eighties, "finding my occasions took me so often to London," he retained as winter quarters the Dover Street house vacated by the death of his last surviving son.

His "occasions" took him into the confidence of Queen Anne's two supreme public servants. One was Sidney, Lord Godolphin, treasurer of England, and his remarkable wife, of whom Evelyn became a deeply valued friend and biographer. (Eventually, the two families were formally joined when Evelyn's grandson married Godolphin's niece.) Through Godolphin, Evelyn met John Churchill, duke of Marlborough and commander-in-chief of England's armed forces. With Marlborough as diplomat and soldier, and Godolphin as director of domestic affairs, the two lifelong friends maintained close to complete control over national policy during the first eight years of Queen Anne's reign.

Other occasions took Evelyn to the offices of the omnipresent William Blathwayt, of whom Charles II had said, "He is never in the way and he is never out of the way." Evelyn, lacking the ambition for place that animated most of his contemporaries and supplied from his youth with an adequate competence from the family fortune, was welcomed by this unequalled dispenser of patronage. Many a place-seeker, young Parke included, sought Blathwayt as an ideal patron. He was a phenomenal collector of offices for himself; like an Indian goddess with multiple arms on each side, he achieved extraordinary effects by rarely revealing what the right and left arms were doing in coordination.

Evelyn's occasions, moreover, were by no means confined to government affairs. He was one of the founders of the Royal Society and thoroughly at home in intellectual circles, whether among the scientists who clustered around Newton or the philosophers who clustered around Locke. After the death of Queen Mary in 1695, when Godolphin named Evelyn treasurer of the naval hospital built at Greenwich in her memory, he worked closely with the age's foremost architect, Sir Christopher Wren, rebuilder of London in the years following the Great Fire of 1666. With such middle-level posts as this, Evelyn was entirely content.

From the standpoint of Parke and others concerned with American colonization, Evelyn's most relevant appointment occurred when Godolphin, in 1671, put him on the Council of Trade and Plantations. Evelyn's diary describes the board's meeting place and the persons and personages, some of them members of the just-established Lords Proprietors of Carolina, who were present when he was sworn in on that twenty-sixth day of May:

> Meeting att *Queenes Street* at the Earl of Bristol's house (which we had lately taken, & furnish'd with rich hangings of the Kings, 7 roomes on a floore with a long Gallery, Gardens &c:) The Duke of Buckingham, E: of Lauderdail, L: Culpeper, Sir Geo: Carteret Vice-Chamberlaine & my selfe, had our Oathes given us by the Earle of Sandwich our President. . . . Then we tooke all our Places in the Council Chamber at the board: The roome very large, & furnished with the Atlases, Mapps, Charts, Globes &c: Then came the Lord Keeper Sir Orlando Bridgeman, E: of Arlington Pr: Secretary of State: Lord Ashley, Mr. Treasurer [and others] . . . who were all Sworne some dayes before: being all set, our Patent was read . . . & then the additional Patent, in which was recited this new establishment.[5]

Parke and his sisters lived in the midst of their ramified cousinry until the winter of 1672–73, when the Long Ditton vestry's register shows that on the second day of January, Rebecca Parke, Gentlewoman, was buried within the Church. "Uxor Mt^re Parke de Virginia Adv: Sepult: in templo."

Daniel Parke, Sr., must have come over as soon as word of his wife's death reached him, for at its session of September 10, 1674, Virginia's York County court recognized 1,550 headrights as accruing to him on his return. A headright, entitling the holder to fifty acres of land, was payable to anyone who in turn had paid passage money for a new settler. Such immigrants usually indentured themselves as servants to established residents—frequently the man who had advanced the fare—for an agreed number of years, thereby repaying the money paid for their passage. In the list of names of

The Evelyn family founder's monument, commemorating George
Evelyn (1526–1603), his two wives, and twenty-four children in the
Evelyn Chapel, St. John's Church, Wotten, Surrey.—*Photograph by
the author, print by Asman*

Meliora Retinete.

μίλου τὰς Εἰκόνας, τῆς ἀρετῆς ὑπόμνημα
μᾶλλον ἢ τῦ σώματος, καταλιπεῖν

A. Nanteüil   I IOK: Πρ∘ς N:κ   delineabat⊕Venl

John Evelyn the Diarist (1620–1706). Engraved in 1650 by Robert
Nanteuil (1623/5–1678).—*National Gallery of Art, Washington, D.C.,
Rosenwald Collection*

those whose passages Parke had paid on this voyage is a notation of "my son Daniel, at my last coming in." The latter's three sisters had remained in England, but he and his father evidently returned together.

The senior Parke could not have foreseen that almost immediately thereafter the Virginia Assembly would send him back to London on colony business. From 1675 to 1677, during the whole of Bacon's Rebellion, he was away; and his Queen's Creek plantation suffered considerable damage as Nathaniel Bacon fought his way down the peninsula to capture and set fire to Jamestown. Did Parke take the boy back to England with him? It seems probable, for if not, who took care of him while his father was gone? There is no record.

The elder Parke had been appointed to the Governor's Council in 1670; his present trip was as a member of a delegation sent by the Virginia Assembly to protest Charles II's recent grant of all of Virginia, except the Northern Neck, which he had already alienated, to two of his favorite courtiers, the Lords Arlington and Culpeper. The chairman of the delegation was Thomas Ludwell, the highest Virginia official short of the governor: he was secretary of the colony and president of the Council.* The delegation's mission was the more delicate because of two subtly conflicting colonial policies that currently coexisted at Whitehall.

The Stuart kings viewed their American lands as a resource from which to reward those who had accomplished the restoration and those whom they had subsequently found congenial at court. The many royal grants included that to Charles's brother, the Duke of York, when New Amsterdam was renamed New York at the close of the Dutch wars; the gift of Pennsylvania to William Penn in recognition of the funds advanced to the royalist cause by his father the admiral; the creation of Maryland for the Baltimore family as a tribute to their Catholic conversion; the conveyance of Carolina to the

---

*The secretaryship was tightly retained: Thomas's brother Philip Ludwell was designated his interim deputy.

Lords Proprietors; the allotment in Virginia of the Northern Neck, currently held by the Fairfaxes;* and the latest award to Arlington and Culpeper.

But while recognizing the King's right to dispose of his territories at will, his ministers were dismayed by these divestments. They were concerned alike by the decrease they caused in the security of England's overseas possessions at a time when New World rivalry with France was growing, and by the relinquishment of resources and revenues that until now had been available to the Crown and the nation. Instead of dissipating English gains from the Age of Discovery in personal rewards, they held, it was necessary to revise and royalize the colonial government structure, bringing all lands under unified crown management. Whenever an opportunity offered, they saw to it that appointments as chief governors and captains general of the colonies went to men of military experience, who were supported in office by English regiments rather than left dependent on local militia.

When members of the Virginia delegation to protest the King's most recent generosity returned from their mission in 1677, they brought with them the welcome news that the ministers had to a considerable extent carried their point. The two new recipients in Virginia had been induced to give up their claims to the granted lands, though retaining the income from taxes and fees raised from them. The pleased Assembly offered congratulations to the mission, and somewhat later a still more favorable result was reported: Culpeper bought out Arlington and settled for a twenty-year annuity from Virginia.

Neither Ludwell nor Parke, however, had long to bask in the public approval: Thomas Ludwell died in October 1678; and Daniel Parke, Sr., who succeeded him as secretary and simultaneously served as treasurer of Virginia, lived only until the spring of 1679.

---

*Taxes received by the colony from this land were now a perquisite of the Fairfax family, acquired through marriage with Lord Culpeper's only daughter. Their payment continued until the American Revolution.

Chapter 3

The Family's London Merchant

DURING his father's settlement of his mother's affairs, if not earlier in connection with remittances to her from Virginia, young Parke must frequently have been in the offices of Messrs. Perry & Lane, the London firm that handled most of the family's American tobacco shipments and orders for English goods.[1] For close to a century since the mid-1660s the successive chief figures in this business were the grandfather Micajah Perry, his son Richard, and his grandson, a second Micajah. With Thomas Lane as a durable partner throughout that long interval, they did business for or with the Parkes.

The City of London was in many ways a place apart. Unlike the rest of the country, and unlike the other boroughs that gathered to form the metropolis, municipal power in the City was exercised in direct response to the desires of its economic components, the chartered companies. These descendants of the medieval guilds, representing the City's merchants and the practitioners of its many trades, were united in the Guildhall. No one who was not a guild member could ply his trade in the City; and, with occasional short-lived exceptions, all these freemen had a vote. So the election of a mayor, an alderman, or a sheriff represented the liveried companies' majority view.

London is so old that in many City buildings, Roman mosaics lie below their lowest levels. For a long time, in the more than millennium and a half of London history, the chief functions of the town concerned the commodities shown by the names of its streets—Bread Street, Wool Street, Milk Street, the Poultry, Cornhill, Cheapside—though not the Billingsgate market where the fish came in. The stately halls of the great companies were close to their members' shops, with the Guildhall at a central point among them. But by the latter years of the seventeenth century, the pivot of City life had swung a little southeast, to the area where eight central thoroughfares intersect, lined with institutions related to banking, finance, insurance, and overseas trade. The signs on the doors of the Poultry as it approaches the intersection ceased to advertise feathered merchandise; and the opposite entrance of Lombard Street no longer recalled the coming of the North Italian refugees—they had remained to become important financiers.

For almost a century the Royal Exchange had stood where Threadneedle Street and Cornhill form a point at the multiple intersection. The original building, destroyed in the Great Fire of 1666 but quickly replaced, had been erected during Elizabeth's reign by the munificent Sir Thomas Gresham to compete with the Antwerp Bourse, where he and his father before him had long served the borrowing requirements of English royalty. Of much more recent date was the Bank of England, to the right of the Exchange and across the street. Founded in 1695, it had first been lodged in the Old Mercer's Hall but soon displayed architecture of its own; it eventually presented the facade that now dominates the intersection.

It was in 1739, the year that the grandson Micajah Perry was Lord Mayor, that the cornerstone was laid for the Mansion House where the City's government has since been lodged. The administrative duties of this government ranged from care of the Thames and maintenance of the City's water supply to the holding of fairs, regulation of ale houses, enforcement of the curfew, and responsibility for the City's defense.

The pomp and ceremony of the companies brought color to the streets. When the sovereign came in procession to St. Paul's Cathedral for celebration of a royal wedding or a military victory, the parade halted at the City's Temple Bar on its way from Westminster. There it was met by the Lord Mayor, his chief officials, and the liveried members of the various companies, mounted and in full panoply, to admit the arrivals. Together they completed their passage, over the street named Fleet after a long-vanished river, to the great edifice on Ludgate Hill, glorious in Gothic before the Great Fire of 1666, glorious in the design of Sir Christopher Wren thereafter.

Such spectacles were sporadic; but for decades after Parliament required the sovereign to view each incoming London mayor, the annual Lord Mayor's Day, November 9, was a day to which even the lowest apprentice could reliably look forward. This time, the procession moved from the City to Westminster, and the robed dignitaries were rowed upriver in barges whose decoration far exceeded the effect possible on a narrow city street. The people of all London packed dockside vantage points to see it.

In this setting the firm headed by the senior Perry illustrated the City's new interests. He lived in the Aldgate Ward; the Bank was to the east of him, St. Paul's was to the west. Among the innumerable coffee houses in between was Edward Lloyd's, where he and his clients could follow the news of commercial gains and losses of the ships on the high seas which carried much of their commerce, and shudder together when the Lutine bell announced a shipwreck or a capture. The elder Micajah was a parishioner of St. Mary le Bow in Cheapside, where the Bow bells were rung each evening at nine o'clock to announce that the merchants were closing their places of business. In 1663, his marriage papers identified him as "haberdasher, about 23," and his bride as Ann Owen, daughter of Dr. Richard Owen, a rising member of the Haberdashers Company. Toward the end of William III's reign, Perry reached an affluence that justified his petition for a coat of arms, citing his descent from the Perrys of Devonshire.* The description of the arms he received from the Garter King at Arms in July 1701 was:

*Now and previously, I have been generously guided through the mysteries of heraldry by Michael Maclagan, C.V.O., F.S.A., former Richmond Herald at the College of Arms in London. I am correspondingly grateful.

LORD MAYORS SHEW at LONDON, *Annually on Nov.9.*

The PROCESSION by WATER

River Pageant, on the annual Lord Mayor's Day, London. The mayor and chief officers of the liveried companies of the City, wearing full regalia and in barges draped with the various companies' colors, were rowed up the Thames for a formal appearance at Westminster.—*Guildhall Library, London*

Per cross Or and Sa. on a bend Gu. cotised Erm., three lions pass. gard. Arg. Crest—A hind's head erased ppr., gorged with a coronet Or, in the mouth a branch of pear tree ppr., fructed Or.[2]

The firm of Perry & Lane went from strength to strength. Its leading members belonged to one of the twelve major associations among the several score of companies of various size and date— from apothecaries to vintners—who regulated the conditions under which their particular type of business was carried on. They also funded a range of charities, supporting school foundations, the apprenticing of boys ready to go to work, and maintenance of the poor.

Of the twelve associations, the Mercers were the leaders. In earlier days, English overseas merchants had concentrated on exports of their countrymen's wool: first as raw wool; then as rough material suitable for clothing for the common man; and latterly as broadcloth for fine gentlemen, its texture smoothed to the requirements of a billiard table with the teazles that grew wild in the West Country.

To Mr. Micajah Perry of London Merchant
This Map of VIRGINIA &c.
is humbly Dedicated and Presented
Thornton,

Micajah Perry's Coat of Arms. John Thornton, the cartographer, dedicated "A New Map of Virginia, Maryland, Pensilvania, New Jersey, Part of New York and Carolina," produced around 1706, to Micajah Perry, the Parkes' agent in London. The cartouche contains a version of Perry's arms.
—*Colonial Williamsburg Foundation*

Now, from ships anchored in midstream in the Thames (docks that could hold back enough water to keep ships of ocean-going size afloat at ebb tide were slow in developing), the Tenderers Company unloaded goods from around the globe: wine, sherry, and port from southwest Europe; spices, pearls, and gems from the Far East; sugar from the Caribbean; tobacco and indigo from Virginia, Maryland, and South Carolina; tall masts, ships stores for the navy, and fish from the northern American mainland and the Great Banks off the Canadian coast.

In England, in the domestic balance of power, trade and finance were gaining influence over the holding of land. More and more loudly, country squires grumbled over the importance of "the money men" in national affairs; and City-centered Whigs became more and more confident as High Tories in the counties became shrill.

During the first half of the eighteenth century, the Perry grandson Micajah became a featured actor on the City scene, rising from public office to public office; and the Virginia Parkes were still one of the Perry clients because of the interminable litigation that contested Daniel Parke II's will. Young Micajah lived in the street called St. Mary Axe, connecting Leadenhall and Houndsditch, northeast of the Bank. During his term as Lord Mayor his residence had a fortuitous convenience in respect to one of his ceremonial duties. The church of St. Andrew Undershaft was only yards from his home.* In the church was an elaborate effigy of John Stow, a member of the Merchant Taylors Company before he gave up his trade to become the great Tudor antiquary and historian. It showed him seated at a table, quill in hand, about to write his *Survey of London*. The quill was

*This church had its name from a very ancient maypole ceremony formerly held there, which used for its pole a shaft taller than the church's steeple. Although lying at the very edge of disaster, the church survived the Great Fire, but the shaft was burned earlier. It hung on the side of the church when not in use, and people came to marvel at its length. One of the Puritan open-air preachers at St. Paul's Cross told the congregation that the shaft had become an idol and should be destroyed. It was sawn up—perhaps into fireplace lengths.

a real one, and each year one of the Lord Mayor's formal functions was to replace the old quill with a new instrument.

Starting as a master liveryman in the Haberdashers, the younger Micajah, in 1727–1728, was elected both alderman of his ward and one of three Whig M.P.'s who easily outbalanced the lone Tory on the City's Parliamentary delegation. In 1734–1735 he was chosen one of London's sheriffs, and on Michelmas Day 1738 he became the City's Lord Mayor, with an annual salary of £4,000.[3] In 1739, he laid the Mansion House cornerstone. Until a disastrous fire in 1846, the Haberdasher's Hall displayed his full-length portrait.

The economic life of a colonial agent was rarely easy. There was a difference between the assumptions of English gentry, who rented their acres to farming tenants and lived on the rents, and the American gentry, who managed their lands, using slave labor, from plantation houses that were their residences. Some of the Americans ran their fields as a business, with personal (and remunerative) attention to details; others hired overseers and to some extent separated themselves from production problems while enjoying their countryman's life. The Custis family, also a Perry & Lane client, exemplified the business-minded group. If a very good crop year promised a glut of tobacco, John Custis III, on his plantation at the tip of the Eastern Shore peninsula on Chesapeake Bay, contracted for space with the first sea captain to present himself for the autumn fleet bound for London; his hogsheads could thus be sold before prices sank to distressingly low levels. After the Bank of England was founded, the family kept a £2,000 deposit there; the interest enabled the Perrys to take advantage of the discount available to those who paid their customs duties in cash. Most families maintained accounts with firms other than their main agent in order to keep comparative annual records of annual sales and play one firm off against another. In addition to the Perrys and three others in London, the Custises had an agent in Bristol and, after the union of England and Scotland, another in Glasgow.

The shippers who sent their crops to Perry & Lane and other firms were chronically overoptimistic about crop prices and overestimated the annual credits to their account. It was by offsets against such credits that the cost of the long lists of what they expected their merchants to procure and send home to them had to be met— lists for such items as furniture, wallpaper, fashionable clothing, fine wines, and products, like tea, that were unobtainable in the colony.*

In addition to expenditures that often exceeded their credits, the Virginians not infrequently confronted the London firms with bills for unexpected outpayments to be made to third parties among their colonial friends. A letter from William Fitzhugh to Nicholas Hayward of December 19, 1693 is typical:

> Having the opportunity of a good bargain from one Mr. D. Parkes I ventured to draw upon you for £100 sterling. . . . I have not so much money of mine in yr hands, yet by no means would have the same protested therefore have sent inclosed towards making up the sum good sure bills as I think of Willis upon Perry & Lane for £7 sterling. I believe I shall be able to send you more bills speedily.[4]

The business transactions were thus rather loosely connected. In addition to dealings of strictly business character, London firms undertook other responsibilities on behalf of their clients, some of which proved onerous. A goodly number of Virginia boys were sent to England for their education without having relatives, as Parke did, who lived in or near London; the merchants frequently served in loco parentis while they were there, providing living arrangements, experience in business, or general oversight and counsel. The fourth John Custis spent over six years of his youth in England in the care of a merchant known as "Old Mr. Baily." His grandfather's will had not only stipulated that the profit on the labor of fourteen slaves be

---

*In the selection of fabrics, help was often solicited from agents' wives, on the grounds that "Womens fancies in things of this nature exceeds that of mens."

used for his early education in Virginia, but included funding for higher studies in England afterwards. He lived in quarters provided by Perry & Lane. Robert Carter, the future "King" Carter of Corotoman, spent six years of his youth in England in the oversight of a merchant and sent over all five of his own sons for study in charge of William Dawkins, one of his London agents. (He had considered Perry & Lane but concluded that "old Mr. Perry is too much a senior for such a business.") William Byrd II arrived at his grandfather's house in Essex at the age of seven; he was first put in the excellent Felsted Grammar School, and then traveled in Holland. Perry & Lane took him into the firm for two years of business experience before he went on to legal studies in the Middle Temple. When such boys got themselves into scrapes, the family's chief merchant usually did his best to extricate them.

Even the boys' elders sought intercessory help from their firms, especially for influence with public officials who had grown heartily tired of colonial complaints. And from time to time, when briefly in London, they too lodged with the Perrys. In 1684–1685, for instance, Parke and his recent bride, Jane Ludwell, did so. The parish register of St. Catherine Cree (only a block from St. Andrew Undershaft) records their visit, the birth and, two months later, the death of their child, and mentions that the Perrys supplied their accommodations. At the end of October 1684, a power of attorney from Micajah to his brother, Peter, who lived for some time in Virginia, was attested to by Parke during his stay in London.

From the first Micajah's time, the Perry firm had taken a special interest in the Virginia tobacco trade. Found among Byrd's papers was "An Essay on Bulk Tobacco" of 1692, thought to have been written by the elder Micajah Perry; it stresses the advantage to American shippers of having their tobacco leaves stemmed, sorted, and packed into hogsheads before shipment across the Atlantic, rather than sending bales of unsorted bulk as many planters, Byrd included, frequently did. (The poorest quality could be put in the center of the bale, a practice that depressed the price of better grades.)

After testifying before Parliament in support of a law prohibiting bulk shipments, grounding his case on the contribution of bulk shipments to the smuggling trade that dropped off loose tobacco in Scottish and Irish ports, Perry, along with sixty-eight other merchants, signed a public petition to this effect.

But the elder Micajah's interest in America was not confined to the Virginia colony and its tobacco. Around the turn of the century he was also engaged in procuring building materials for the new construction at Williamsburg—first for the construction of the College of William and Mary and then for the new capitol. He became a financial supporter of the college, making a personal contribution of £50. It is very likely that he visited Virginia more than once. His application for permission to go there in 1701 is on file in the papers of the Privy Council, and his brother Peter lived in York County for some years. He also had business connections in Pennsylvania and New York.

In 1706 William Byrd II had succeeded to his late father's post as receiver general of the royal revenues of the colony, a post that brought the holder 3½ percent of the receipts, raised to 5 percent before he relinquished his tenure on his return to England as Virginia's agent. Such a position gave him insight into everyone's affairs, and during 1709–1711, entries in his diary show the subjects on which he wrote to Perry and indicate why the Board of Trade repeatedly sought Perry's advice on nominations for membership in the colonial Council. The board was further indebted to him for the support he brought to its conviction that central administration of the colonies directly under the Crown was a highly desirable alternative to the grants of American holdings to various lords proprietors lavished on courtiers by the Stuart kings.

Just as the families' merchants did their best to extract boys who got themselves into trouble, they aided the boys' elders who sought favors of various kinds, especially for influence with public officials. In 1703, after Queen Anne's accession, the Perrys presented a petition from Parke to the Lords of Trade requesting them to supply a portrait of Her Majesty and a device carved with the royal coat of arms for use by the government of Virginia. And, in the last years of Parke's life, the firm assiduously represented his political interests during his accumulating difficulties in the Leeward Islands governorship.

As the new century rolled on, however, imbalances in transatlantic payments reached unmanageable proportions. Tobacco production, some 15 million pounds in the late 1660s, swelled above 28 million by the 1680s, and a long decline in prices and profitability for the London merchants began. After the union of England and Scotland in 1707, Glasgow's advantages as a seaport far closer to the tobacco-growing lands, with corresponding savings in shipping costs and shipping time, also began to make itself felt in London.

The political successes of Micajah Perry the younger began to be paralleled by economic stringencies. Whereas in earlier years, a newspaper account of the marriage of his sister described the bride as "a young lady of £10,000 fortune," by midcentury the unstable economics of the tobacco trade forced Perry & Lane and other respected firms to declare bankruptcy. The humiliation of the failure must have affected this Micajah physically: when he retired as alderman in 1746 the document was signed only with his mark; and during his final years the Haberdashers Company, as part of its obligation to look after its own, contributed an annual £200 to his support and care.

Chapter 4

Introduction to Public Life

ONCE the Parkes, father and son, were back in Virginia, it was time for the father to introduce his son to the colonial community. The boy was now about fifteen, old enough to understand what was going on during the occasions when his parent's duties made him an official participant in public life.

Virginia was still a land of first beginnings, and the assumptions that many colonists had brought with them were in many cases almost ridiculously inconsistent with wilderness life. A fair number of the royalist refugees of the midcentury had come from upper levels of England's class society—some were collateral relatives of the families who lived in imposing houses on landed estates—and even those with humbler origins anticipated the development in America of a similar social structure, perhaps with themselves as ranking members if their dreams of making a fortune came true.

Even the earliest immigrants, in forecasting needs for occupational skills for their western venture, had proposed, in addition to more usual everyday occupations, a number whose output would be required only by families living in the upper ranges of consumption. One of these lists contained thirty-two different trades said to be necessary. The specialists should include not only boatbuilders, ropemakers, metalworkers, gun founders, and farriers—who indeed would be needed—but others whose occupations every man must himself be capable of performing passably well to survive in virgin territory—ploughman, fisherman, fowler, baker, brewer, and builder. And over and above these, a few were named whose skills even at home were confined to quality markets. Newly arrived colonists could get along for quite some time without silk dressers, or pearl drillers, and, most of all, without men who knew how to prepare caviar from sturgeon (even though the fish were plentiful).[1]

Symbolic of such expectations was the great house, Greenspring, built by Governor Sir William Berkeley three miles from Jamestown soon after his arrival as governor in 1642. It was expanded and stood until 1797, when a later owner had it pulled down and replaced by a more contemporary design by Benjamin Latrobe. Latrobe's sketch of the original house remains to show its early appearance; it was ninety-seven feet long and consisted of three very large rooms in a row, with an ell at the far end. The style was Tudor, with huge chimneys and diamond-shaped leaded glass in its windows. The view across fields to the James River was suitably impressive.

As in England, the commonalty built wattle-and-daub houses with stout timber frames or, somewhat later, log cabins on the Scandinavian model. The architectural range gave the social range permanent visibility.

Governor Berkeley was the younger brother of the first Lord Baron of Stratton; the magnificent castle above the Severn from which the Berkeleys took their name had been in possession of the senior branch of the family since feudal times. Greenspring was a small house by comparison, but it was by far the most imposing in the colony. Its midcentury influence as the headquarters of the royalist faction and, subsequently, the seat of Lady Berkeley and the Ludwell family, made it a factor in Virginia politics.

A sketch also exists of a house first called Fairfield, built by the second Lewis Burwell, who was Parke's uncle, on Carter's Creek in Gloucester County. Also in Tudor style, it was far simpler than Greenspring, but its spacious ballroom, with marble mantels, was much admired, and it could readily qualify as a rather sophisticated English manor. So, in the early eighteenth century, could the mansions of Daniel Parke II's sons-in-law: John Custis's homes—the family plantation at Arlington on Virginia's Eastern Shore and the house he built as a widower on Francis Street in Williamsburg; and William Byrd's Westover as he rebuilt it in the early 1730s.

Yet in spite of these grandeurs, the stately homes of Tidewater and the places of public gatherings could be reached only by roads that were no more than tracks, through sand near river courses, over slippery red clay farther inland. Communal labor, levied by the gentlemen justices of the county court, precariously stuffed the worst holes with branches and dirt. Travel on horseback was slow, and vehicular travel, lurching on big-wheeled riding chairs or in cumbersome family coaches, was both more dangerous and slower. After such a journey, cousinly visits to large plantation houses tended to be prolonged.

Gregarious Virginians therefore welcomed their regular opportunities to see each other. The most frequent community gatherings were on Sunday. The Church of England was the established church, and the law required weekly attendance at its services: if this obligation were casually observed, a frequent absentee would be called before the county court to explain. But most people looked forward to being there.

The churches erected in each parish of the settled parts of the colony gave the families living in the immediate locality a social center; the average parish covered approximately ten square miles. They thronged the churchyard for eager chatter, prolonged by a little straggling, especially on the part of the men, when the time came to move indoors to join in the stately responses of the *Book of Common Prayer* and listen in silent accord to the rector's homily. They paid temporal as well as spiritual attention to the announcements read after the second lesson, for these included the publishing of banns for forthcoming marriages and other interesting events; along with notices posted at the mill, they served in place of a newspaper.

Afterward, for an interval terminated only by an increasingly felt need to get home for the midafternoon Sunday dinner, men pontifi-

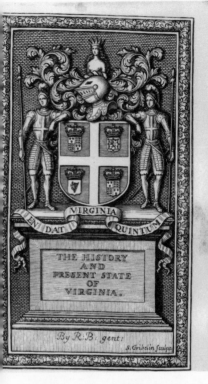

THE

HISTORY

OF

VIRGINIA,

In Four PARTS.

I. The HISTORY of the First Settlement of *Virginia*, and the Government thereof, to the Year 1706.

II. The natural Productions and Conveniencies of the Country, suited to Trade and Improvement.

III. The Native *Indians*, their Religion, Laws, and Customs, in War and Peace.

IV. The present State of the Country, as to the Polity of the Government, and the Improvements of the Land, the 10th of *June* 1720.

By a Native and Inhabitant of the PLACE.

The SECOND EDITION revis'd and enl g'd by the AUTHOR.

LONDON:

Printed for F. FAYRAM and J. CLARKE at the *Royal-Exchange*, and T. BICKERTON in *Pater-Noster-Row*, 1722.

"Virginia Offers a Fifth Crown." Motto on coat of arms of original Virginia Company, shown here as it appears on title page of Robert Beverley's *History and Present State of Virginia* (1705).—*Colonial Williamsburg Foundation*

Greenspring. The great house of early Virginia was built some three miles from Jamestown by Governor Sir William Berkeley soon after his arrival in the 1640s. Philip Ludwell II, Parke's uncle, became the next proprietor on his marriage to Berkeley's widow. Benjamin H. Latrobe (1764–1820) painted this watercolor when he visited the site.
—*Maryland Historical Society*

cated and women chirruped in further exchange of news, views, and gossip. Youthful flirtations were advanced, and observed. Shrewd estimates assessing the horseflesh present mingled with forecasts of tobacco prices, wheat prospects, land sales. The ranking families exchanged items of interest received in their latest letters from London. Voters considered and consulted each other on likely candidates for the county's next election of its two representatives to sit in the General Assembly at Jamestown.

The absence of a bishop in Virginia caused the churches to be run by vestries of twelve men. In a new parish, the first twelve were elected by the male citizens of the parish. After the Vestries Act of 1662, established vestries were self-perpetuating. Like the election of burgesses, the early viva voce voting by which selections were made was frequently disorderly. After the turn of the century, as a means of "avoiding all tumult and confusion, which usually happens on such occasions," the Governor's Council laid down exact rules to be observed by the sheriff when taking a poll for vestrymen. The new system, by requiring the use of lists, foreshadowed later voting by secret ballot. It undoubtedly quieted the electoral scene; it also eliminated much of the pungent humor exchanged by hecklers under the previous system.

An important function of the vestrymen, in addition to their specifically ecclesiastical duties, such as finding a qualified minister, maintaining church property, etc., was to exercise public responsibility for the care of the parish poor, the indigent sick, and the many orphans whom disease, accident, and the rough life of the frontier left without kinsmen to support, oversee, and eventually apprentice them. The apprenticeship agreement is illustrated by the case of young Richard Allen.

First securing the consent of his mother, the Bruton vestry bound Richard to Mr. William Bernard, to serve him until he was twenty-one. At the same time, they bound his master to give the boy three years of schooling, beginning at about age twelve, and to agree with the churchwardens to provide him with clothing, meat and drink, washing and lodging, and "all such allowances as is to his Due, according to the Custom of this Country."

To cover the costs of these public duties, the salaries of the rectors, and obligations under any existing contracts for building or repair of church properties, the vestrymen laid tithes for whose payment all parishioners were liable. Their day-to-day decisions were carried out by two churchwardens, who were elected annually from their number for one-year terms.

For over twenty years, the senior Parke was an active vestryman. His holdings on York River were originally part of Marston Parish, established, with a wooden church, in 1654. The Middle Plantation settlement had been laid out in 1632, and a church built there. In 1644 this settlement and a parish called Harrop in James City County merged to form Middletown Parish, and in 1674, Marston and Middletown united to form Bruton Parish.* Bruton thus comprised a broad strip of land that reached all the way across the peninsula between the York and the James rivers.

The first entry in the earliest surviving Bruton parish book starts with the names of the vestrymen present on April 18, 1674; the list is topped by the name of "The Honourable Coll: Daniel Parke," and the first item of completed business records repayment to him and the Honourable Thomas Ludwell of money they had advanced for the purchase of a parish glebe.

The following November this vestry took a bold decision: since the wooden churches in the parish were in bad repair, they should be replaced by a single new church, built of brick and located in Middle Plantation. Thomas Ludwell, Daniel Parke, and Major John Page had already pledged support for the project; the churchwardens were now instructed to raise further "subscriptions of free donations," and John Page immediately offered an additional £20, together with a gift of land "sufficient for the Church and Church Yard." Thus

---

*The name was chosen in honor of the English parish in Somerset from which Governor Berkeley and the Ludwell family came.

stimulated, Rowland Jones, an Oxford man who had been serving as the church's clerk, and others with him, pledged £5 each. Mr. Jones became the church's rector.

Daniel Parke, Sr., had recently started several businesses, among them a shipyard and a brick factory. Some bricks used by the colonists were imported as ballast; more were locally made in imported molds; and still others were simply fired after being shaped from stiff red clay. His brickyard supplied needed materials for the new buildings.

By June 1679 the vestry had signed a contract with a builder who agreed to transform their completed plans into a church at a price of £350. But, as frequently happened, trouble developed between the vestry and the contractor. In 1681 a new agreement was made with a new builder, and construction was resumed. By November 29, 1683, the vestry was able to set January 6, 1684, Epiphany Sunday, for the ceremony of dedication: the clerk was instructed to "sett up notice at ye Mill" to inform parishioners.

The second most frequent public occasion for a community gathering was the monthly meeting of the York County court. In each county, the governor appointed eight or nine justices of the peace, who were chosen by the Lords of Trade and Plantations either from lists of suitable persons that the governor had prepared or by a combination of his list with requests from interested patrons. In 1653, Parke was named a gentleman justice for York; over the next quarter of a century he was a regular attendant at sessions.

During that entire time, the county did not have a court house. At first, the court met at one of the larger homes such as Parke's; then, beginning in 1679–1680, it sat either at the "French ordinary" or nearby at the Half-Way House, two taverns centrally located on the road connecting York County with Martin's Hundred in James City County. It was only in 1691, when an act of the Assembly prescribed the laying out of a number of ports, that the justices provided a building. A fifty-acre tract on the York River was then divided into half-acre lots, and various families, such as the Ludwells, made purchases. The hamlet was named Yorktown.

Governor Francis Nicholson took a helpful interest in the start of the project: he transferred three of the lots he had bought for use by the present schoolmaster and, subsequently, such persons as should teach school with the approbation and allowance of the court. He pledged a further £20 if, within two years, a brick church were built at the town. And when he initiated a local postal service, he used Yorktown as its center; it permitted a settler, on payment of three cents, to send a message, limited to a single sheet of letter-paper, for a distance not to exceed eighty miles.

As a result of all this activity, at its March session of 1697–98 the court was able to order the county's sheriff to remove to Yorktown before the next court day the standard of the county and all other moveable implements and materials.

The agenda of the county court included exercise of all the functions of government, executive, legislative, and judicial, that the county required. Its executive officer was the county sheriff—a post Parke filled for the year 1659—who saw to it that the court's judgments were carried out and its ordinances put into effect. In 1662, when it was decided that the county should set up official standards of weights and measures, it was Parke who ordered a set of each of these, plus an iron with which to mark pewter weights and pewter pots, and scales to weigh 1,200 pounds accurately to be used to test people's stillyards.[2]

The justices required compliance with colony-wide regulations regarding the planting and harvesting of tobacco in years of price-cutting gluts. They also assigned property owners responsibility for the maintenance of roads and bridges and fixed prices to be charged for both storage space in warehouses and for meals and lodging in inns and ordinaries. There had been a saying among the burgesses who attended meetings of the colonial Assembly that the tavern-keepers of Jamestown "operated their ordinaries at extra-ordinary rates." They laid taxes to cover county expenditures and summoned individuals to explain such negligences as failure to list themselves as taxable, or to acknowledge ownership of personal property, such as a coach, on which special taxes were laid. They heard cases brought by citizens against each other on such subjects as failure to pay a debt or honor a contract: if a plaintiff were dissatisfied with the quality of work done, say in replacing a roof, the court appointed unprejudiced viewers to advise it on the roof's condition.

The justices also punished breaches of the moral code in cases such as theft or adultery, though major crimes, such as murder, were tried by the General Court at the capital.

Persons summoned as witnesses in the trials scheduled for a given session were strictly required to be present. An explanation addressed to the justices for a failure to attend the trial of a case in 1669 conveys the poignancy of life and death on the frontier:

> Honll Gentlemen
>
> I am necessitated to intercede in the halfe of Doctor Haddon in case of his non appearance at your court . . . since the occasion which caused his absence proceeds from . . . my daughters sickness . . . I shall leave it to you to judge . . . whether on such an occasion as this where the life or death of your child in probability depends that latitude may not be allowed wch in another case may be judged intolerable. . .
>
> Your most humble servant
Peter Jennings[3]

As young Parke mingled with the attendance on court days he could meet and observe a fairly complete cross section of the community: the justices themselves; the attorneys, plaintiffs, defendants, and witnesses for the scheduled trials; individuals determined to state their approval of or opposition to proposals the justices were considering in respect to roads, prices, assessments, etc.; farmers who had agreed to meet with each other to bargain over land, crops, slaves, stock, and the like; and some who came simply to keep up with what was going on, and to view the trials as theater.

And theater it frequently was, to judge by some of the starkly condensed minutes of the court on some of the occasions when the senior Parke was present.* For instance:

• Although the unlettered John Horsington signed his depositions with a mark, over the course of time he was accepted and identified in court records as a gentleman. The court, when determining facts, called on him fairly frequently and was inclined to give weight to his sworn statements: he was a man who seemed to know what went on among the colony's indentured population. Sometimes his inquiries were met with pert answers. One of his depositions, in 1657, related to the bastard child fathered by one of Parke's indentured servants on one of Parke's Negro slaves. Horsington reported:

> she said that if they were parted she would come to him by night or by day for where love could not goe itt would creepe att another time I being att Robert Taylor his house where the sd Sarah did live the sd Robert Taylor coming home hee sd to Sarah . . . there is a sweet clamour abroad for people say that I dandle you on my knee & kisse you. Itt is noe matter said Sarah if you havt the Devill take you if you doe not.[4]

• In October 1661 the court investigated the death of one Thomas Lees. Parke had already taken a vivid deposition of John Symmons, who said:

> that going for Oysters . . . [my Masters] boat, and one Thomas Lees with mee who was a servant . . . also and being uppon the Creeke a little below the Oystershell bancke . . . wee fell out about Rowing and hee told mee hee would throw mee overboard for my uncles sake, . . . and soe hee did & did hold

*Peter V. Bergstrom, of the Colonial Williamsburg Foundation's York County Project, generously pointed out the references to both father and son in the public records of the colony.

mee by the legg till I was almost stifled and then hee let mee goe and presently I did see him in the water behind mee & I swamme to the shoare & what became of him I know not.[5]

A jury was summoned for an inquest: Parke charged them "to inquire how thomas leea came by his casual death." The jury reported that "wee . . . have found his body aforesaid within High water marke in York River & viewed him fully and doe find upon our oathes that his death was accidental." Correspondingly, the court delivered its verdict: "wee find the said Thomas Leea was drowned by accident and not wilfully."[6]

• In 1662 John Horsington appeared in another role than that of an expert witness. Tavern frequenters in their cups, if they had proved offensive, could be summoned to make a public apology for what they had said; that spring, Horsington was forced to titillate listeners by offering a profuse public recantation:*

To all Christian people whom this shall concern Know yee that I John Horsington being at Mr foliotts house in Company with Mr Daniell Wild and some other neighbours there at that time hapned some words of difference to arise betwixt the said Wild and I the said Horsongton amongst which words it appeareth by sufficyent testimony though I dow not well remember it that I the said Horsington did call the said Wild perjured fellow and said I would prove him 2 for the which although at that present I was not altogether myselfe yet I hereby ackhowledg myselfe heartily sorry for soe undeservedly calling the said Wild perjured fellow hee being a very honest man and loving neighbour for ought I ever knew found or anyway able to justify to the Contrary and I am very willing and freely consent that this my submission be Recorded in Yorke Court and further I obleige my selfe to pay all Costs of Court.[7]

*Horsington's lapse caused embarrassment to the justices, for Daniel Wild was the county's high sheriff.

Wild's duties frequently included punishment of mothers of bastard children. In August 1661 Parke's servant, Elizabeth Holloway, having, to the "offense against Almighty God," given birth to such a child by another of Parke's servants, received a sentence of ten stripes on her bared back and an obligation to pay her master a fine, either in service or in money, at the expiration of her indenture. But Elizabeth and a friend in the same condition got away unpunished; having recovered them, the court came back to the case the next August and assigned Parke and another justice to view execution of the sentence.[8]

Parke's presence in court as a justice was not infrequently varied by his appearance as a plaintiff or a defendant. Most of the cases in which he was a contestant had to do with debts owed to or by him, either in pounds of tobacco or in pounds sterling. Two of the larger suits in 1666 concerned nonperformance under contracts to build a house. In April, the executor of the late Robert Bourne, a long time friend of Parke, appeared, seeking a court ruling as to whether he had obligations to a builder for completing considerable work on a house that had formerly belonged to Parke; the sum at issue was 666 pounds of tobacco at 4½ pence per pound.[9]

In November, Parke himself sued one William Belvin for nonperformance on another house; his complaint was sustained. (This house, to be thirty feet long, was a considerable undertaking. Parke may have ordered it in compliance with an Assembly call for prominent citizens to build houses of that length—and twenty feet wide, with a roof pitch of fifteen feet—at Jamestown to give a more prepossessing appearance to the capital.)[10]

The last case in which the name of the senior Parke occurs is a tantalizing reference on July 22, 1671, indicating that a falling out had occurred between him and one of his in-laws: he and a Captain Evelin agreed to a continuance, with the trial postponed until November 21. A second postponement was then announced, after which there is no further word. Perhaps the matter continued to drag on until Parke left for London on the news of Rebecca's death. Perhaps—and more likely—the two contestants reached a settlement of the matter out of court. But what was the contested issue?

In this fashion, at one court day or another, all of the misdoings of the community from mayhem to miscegenation, from slander to stealing, were alleged and either substantiated or declared unproven. An eager audience listened while the court sat and argued out-of-doors about the justice of its verdicts as soon as the session was over. Every county court had, and used, its jail, its pillory, its stocks, its ducking stool, and, on occasion, its gallows.

The theater supplied by the court's regular monthly meetings was generally exceeded in rowdiness at election times. The popular choices that selected the county's two representatives in the House of Burgesses were made on a day when the court met, and at its place of meeting. Attendance was usually augmented by voteless citizens as well as by the candidates, their agents, and the men who were entitled to vote. (The rolls listed all freeholders and, as time went on, all householders too.) The crowd was enlarged by the expectation that the candidates would supply liquid refreshment; only in the last year of the century was a law passed declaring that no candidate for burgess "shall directly or indirectly by any ways or means . . . give . . . to any person or persons haveing voice or vote in such election any money, meat, drink or provision, or make any present, gift, reward or entertainment . . . in order to procure the vote . . . of such person . . . for . . . election to be a burgess."[11] Even then it was an ineffective law.

An election usually began either inside the courthouse or on the steps outdoors if the crowd could not be accommodated in the building where the court met. If they were presenting themselves in a first candidacy, candidates described what they would do if elected; if they were incumbents, they extolled what they had done and presented their future plans. Then the sheriff called on each voter on his roll, requiring oaths to be taken in cases of questioned eligibility. The person called on stood up and named his preference; the candidate he named stood up and bowed a grateful acknowledgment of the favor. Sheriff and onlookers alike kept tabs, amid mounting tension and excitement if a race proved close. Winners were declared and subsequently certified. Leftover treats did not go to waste, and during the entire proceeding, fisticuffs were frequent.

Daniel Parke, Sr., had been a burgess in 1663 before his son was born, but after 1670 his appointment as a member of the Governor's Council elevated him to the upper house. As the largest landholder in York County, however, his interest in the quality of the county's representation in the Assembly insured his presence at the hustings.

For the Parkes, as for others of their rank in Virginia, the most festive of the occasions that brought people together were the semiannual meetings of the Assembly and General Court at Jamestown in spring and fall. In the latter 1670s the town, still largely unrestored after its destruction in Bacon's Rebellion, was a ghost slowly rising from the ashes of its statehouse, its church, and several of its few important houses. Consequently, accommodations were far from sufficient. Every family that lived there had a houseful of guests, and the revived taverns were bulging. Until the new statehouse was finished in 1686, space for the legislative sessions had to be rented: the burgesses sat in the Great Hall of William Sherwood's house, where the owner supplied firewood, candles, and service over and beyond the agreed rent for the premises.

During these occasions, rising young men such as Daniel Parke, Jr., suitably presented by their fathers, could meet their peers from other counties and attend balls and parties where their future marriages were astutely planned by their elders—and on occasion otherwise arranged by themselves. Many of the girls married at fourteen, most by sixteen; after eighteen old maidenhood began to stare the remaining virgins in the face. Though May and December were sometimes joined in holy matrimony as a result of these meetings, most of the husbands were only slightly older than their brides.

Horse races enlivened the days, dancing embellished the evenings. Ladies enjoyed their afternoon tea, gentlemen their evening madeira. In doing their best to imitate a London season, men and women wore their most recently imported wardrobes; the women's hairdressers placed curls where curls should be, and the men's all-enveloping wigs, as similar as possible to those affected by the Stuart royalty, were carefully combed into suitable waves and ringlets. Harpsichords were tuned and flutes polished. For tables sparkling with crystal and silver, roe-plump shad were seined on their way to spawning grounds upriver in the spring; and in the fall fowlers took aim at V-shaped skeins of migrating geese, pairs of great white whistling swans, and rising rafts of various wild ducks.

The transfer of the capital from Jamestown to Williamsburg provided further grandeur. King William instructed Governor Nicholson to initiate the building of a house for the governor. After the college and the statehouse were in place, upper-class desire for distinctive style and form was embodied in a 1706 Act of Assembly specifying details—and providing financing—for a Governor's House to be placed at the end of a green that crossed the Duke of Gloucester Street halfway between the two major existing buildings. The burgesses committed themselves to a donation of £3,000 for the erection of a two-story structure measuring fifty-four by forty-eight feet, built of brick, with stone copings on windows and a slate roof. Its dependencies should include a kitchen and stables. Decorative ironwork, glass, lead, stone, slate, and other necessary materials should be imported from England; and local purchases of slaves, horses, carts, and available materials should be made by the overseer of the work, in consultation with the lieutenant governor and Council.

Four years later, progress under this act had been far from satisfactory. On November 24, the overseer of the building was petitioning the Assembly for past due pay. Money had run out, work had stopped, and the overseer had spent his own funds to prevent what had been built from becoming damaged.

The burgesses raised another £1,560 to be applied with "all convenient Expedition," and a further £635 was granted for additions: to construct a walled courtyard at the entrance to the house, fronted by handsome gates; to lay out a garden 250 feet long and 144 wide, enclosed by a brick wall with wooden balustrades, likewise gated; to plant a convenient kitchen garden and orchard; to enclose a pasture, ditched and fenced; and to put up a wooden cattle shed and a poultry house. From the £635, a sum of £250 should be set aside for house furnishings, to be purchased either domestically or in England.

In spite of both of these acts, it was a long time before Virginia's governors were housed as the Assembly directed. The first occupant to live in what some settlers, disgruntled at the ever-rising costs, began to call the Governor's Palace, was Alexander Spotswood, who expedited affairs by moving in on top of the workmen in 1714, and enjoyed the completed structure from 1716 until the end of his tenure six years later.

Meanwhile, a small foretaste of the coming magnificence was enjoyed in the special and spacious pew set aside for the governor at Jamestown's church and later at Bruton: placed at the juncture of chancel and transept, it was like a royal box at a theater, caparisoned in scarlet. On a Sunday morning, the trip from the governor's dwelling to the church became a small procession.

The route of the comparable procession when the governor opened a session of the Assembly was psychologically longer. In London there was both a real and a symbolic distance between palace and parliament; in the colony the legislature was the scene where difficulties—leading occasionally to confrontations between governor and governed—became visible.

A royal governor arrived bearing instructions that he was bound to follow, with reference to laws and orders that both he and the colonists under him were obligated to observe. Though the colonists theoretically brought with them all the rights and privileges that the king's subjects enjoyed at home, the reality of this protection was sometimes challenged. In addition, there were quarrels about the Navigation Acts, which governed transatlantic trade, determining the ports at which ocean-going ships were permitted to call, and levying export and import taxes on the goods they moved. All acts

The "Bodley Plate" of Williamsburg's early public buildings, a copper-plate made about 1740 and identified in Oxford's Bodleian Library in 1929. The top strip shows (center) the east front of the principal building of the College of William and Mary after the fire of 1705, together with Brafferton Hall (left), erected in 1723 as a school for Indians, and the President's House (right), finished in 1732. The second strip shows (left and center) two views of the Capitol finished in 1705 and (right) the Governor's Palace, completed in 1716. The bottom strip depicts Native Americans and Virginia flora and fauna.—*Colonial Williamsburg Foundation*

passed by the Assembly had to bear the signature of the governor and be forwarded to London, where they could be disallowed by the Lords of Trade.

London had a firm hand in naming not only the governor, but the members of his Council. The governor's appointments of such local administrators as surveyors, escheators of land, receivers of royal revenues, and county justices of the peace were subject to London's direction and scrutiny.

Into this framework, governors and the chief men of the colony had to fit. Among those nearest to the governor there were always a few sycophants who could find no wrong in anything he did; but councilmen who had special connections, official or unofficial, with men of power in England—in the hierarchy of the Church of England or among titled families with a long hereditary heritage of land or shorter prominence in the world of City finance—could be independent, even in that inner circle.

In private consultations at the spring and fall meetings, during, say, an afternoon around a well-chosen bottle at Mann's ordinary, or at private dinners after the ladies had withdrawn, friends and factions exchanged their estimates of the acceptability and likely tenure of the current governor. If relations between these substantial citizens and the governor had been deteriorating, the talk might turn to the advisability of sending one or two of their number to England, either privately or officially, by the Assembly, to suggest his removal.

During the last quarter of the seventeenth century, the sending of several such missions led to the practice of naming an agent to live in London and represent the colony. Though the development was by no means identified as such, this amounted to the colonists setting up an unofficial functionary to parallel the official line of communication already existing through the governor. Just as members of the Governor's Council and the House of Burgesses maintained a relationship of social community with the governor—his balls were given and attended with courtesy whether or not discourteous exchanges had occurred in legislative sessions earlier in the day—a socially acceptable Virginian residing in London could quietly negotiate solutions to incipient political problems before they had to be recognized officially. And when things were going well, the agent could be usefully engaged in forwarding mutual economic interests.

William Byrd II, Virginia's first London agent to bear the name, typified the suitable man for this post. Romantics called him the Black Swan of Westover. Manners were at their best when he was seen "cutting a leg," the low formal bow corresponding to a perfectly performed feminine curtsey with which a gentleman responded to a presentation. His body was gracefully built, and he carried himself with the tacit assumption of superiority of the English upper class. With others of the Royal Society, such as the aristocrats whose portraits he commissioned for his gallery at Westover, he moved with an ease that was ambiguous as to whether he was really a colonial or an indigenous member of London's intellectual community. Recent decodings of the secret diaries he kept at various periods of his life, combined with his various and copious correspondence, supply an autobiography of one of the ranking grandees of Virginia.

When describing his idyll at Westover to his lifetime friend Lord Orrery, Byrd sketched a way of life that was happily comprehensible to the owners of the English country houses they both knew so well:

> I have a large family of my own, and my doors are open to every body, yet I have no bills to pay, and half a crown will rest undisturbed in my pocket for many moons together. Like one of the patriarchs, I have my flocks and my herds, my bondsmen and my bondswomen, and every sort of trade amongst my own servants, so that I live in a kind of independence of everyone but Providence. However, this sort of life is without expense, yet it is attended with a great deal of trouble. I must take care to keep all my people to their duty, to set all the springs in motion, and to make everyone draw his equal share to carry the machine forward. But then 'tis an amusement in this silent country and a continual exercise of our patience and economy.[12]

But such grandees could be thorns in the sides of arriving governors. Governor Spotswood, who arrived in 1710, the year after Byrd's appointment to the Council, reported that the Council had reduced the powers of the governor to "a desperate gasp," and placed them under the pressure of "the haughtiness of a Carter, the hypocrisy of a Blair . . . the malice of a Byrd." Let a governor intrude on one of their Edens, and an independent response was quickly forthcoming. Among members of the House of Burgesses, who represented great landowners but also relied on the vote of less affluent men, and who in many cases lived at greater distance from the governor, socially and physically, than members of his Council, such a reaction was even swifter. Few governors were long popular, and after Sir William Berkeley, few of those who actually came to the colony were long tenured. Over the next years, Parke might well have observed the gubernatorial experience as a cautionary tale applicable to his own future.

Daniel Parke, Sr., had only barely enough time to familiarize his heir with the customs of the country before his tenure as secretary and treasurer of the colony, councilman, and vestryman ended suddenly with his death on March 6, 1679. The boy, still not of age, was hurtled into man's estate.

Young Daniel inherited all of his father's lands and slaves. Over and above the York County holdings and some 200 acres in Martin's Hundred Parish, these included between 3,000 and 5,000 acres in New Kent County on the west side of Skimino, the creek that formed the dividing line with York; 3,800 acres along the Pamunkey River in what became known as King William County; and about 1,150 western acres near the Chickahominy River still farther inland.

Under their father's will, the three daughters in England were to receive £1,500 each, either at age eighteen or on the day they married. Money remaining in England from sales of tobacco or earnings from shipping was also to be invested for their benefit.

All three of the girls married into London's business world. Evelyn, the eldest, was married twice, first to a husband whose last name was Humphries, then to Gilbert Pepper, a commissioner for the sick and hurt in Ireland. In 1685 Rebecca became the wife of a widower merchant named John Goddard; the will he drew up as they set out on a trip to Holland provided that if she died en route, a third of his estate should go to her brother, Daniel. The following year saw the wedding of the youngest sister, Jane, to Sampson Sherwood, draper; on this occasion his relative, John Sherwood, grocer, transferred three properties in the family's earlier home in Thurnby, Leicestershire, to Micajah Perry, to be used for the benefit of the newlyweds. Jane also was twice married, the second time to Sampson Sherrard, a silkman, whose uncle, Dr. Sherrard, was a well-known English consul, merchant, and botanist in the Middle East.

Around the end of the century, the Sherrard family was in frequent contact with Parke, who was then in London. In 1700, a Dr. Sherrard, doing business in Smyrna across the Mediterranean, was associated with Parke and two others in a jointly ventured voyage of a ship with cargo bound from London to Virginia. Consigned to the junior Sampson Sherrard, then in the colony, the ship was lost; and long after Parke's death, the Perry firm was still working on the resulting case in the Court of Chancery. Sampson Sherrard lived for some time in Virginia and appears with Jane Parke in the records of York County cases in which she was a participant in Daniel's absence.

By a curious omission in Daniel Parke, Sr.'s will, no guardian was specifically appointed to serve until Daniel, Jr. came of age, but among the Londoners listed as executors-in-trust during his minority, Micajah Perry assumed the role, while in Virginia, Robert Cobb, a vestryman who had been a close friend of his father, did so.[13]

In its essentials the father's will was very simple and conventional, but it contained one unusual feature: inheritances were to be confined to persons either already bearing the name of Parke or adopting it. If his son succeeded him, as became the case, this stipulation would be automatically fulfilled. But in case of a failure of heirs male, the limitation was to apply to the husband and heirs of his eldest daughter. Father Parke had made his name, and he (and eventually his son after him) proposed to see that it endured.[14]

The community respect that the senior Daniel enjoyed was evidenced by a mural tablet, perhaps the first monument in this form to be erected in English America. In the Bruton church dedicated in 1684, in whose building he had been such an active vestryman, the chief interior ornament was this plaque to his memory. Soon after replacement of this church by today's building in 1715, John Custis, widower of Daniel Parke II's elder daughter Frances, asked the vestry's permission to move the plaque to the new sanctuary. It now hangs beside the pulpit in the chancel. The inscription reads:

> Near this Marble Lyes
> ye Honble Daniel Parke
> of ye County of Essex Esq who
> was one of his Ma:ties Counsellers
> and some time Secretary of the
> Collony of Virg:a he Died ye 6th of
> March Anno 1679
> His other felicityes ware Crowned by
> his happy Marridg with Rebbecka
> the daughter of George Evelyn
> of the County of Surry Esq she dyed
> the 2d of January Anno 1672 at Long
> Ditton in ye County of Surry and
> left behind her most
> hopefull progeny

The life of Parke's orphaned son had now to indicate the extent to which that progeny was hopeful.

Chapter 5

The Ludwell Connection

DANIEL Parke, Jr.'s first independent contribution to his political advancement was his marriage in the early 1680s to Jane, daughter of Philip Ludwell II. In view of the frequent collaboration between the fathers of these young people, the union of the two families was a natural development, but it also served young Parke's aims as no other could have done. By this alliance, he grafted himself into a family tree that was adorned with lovely ornaments, each of which represented a governorship already held.

The convention that led seventeenth- and eighteenth-century portrait painters to present very young children in dress that was a diminutive reproduction of the garments worn by their adult sitters had a symbolic significance. For most of those so painted, childhood was brief, with early maturity crowding upon adolescence. At everyone's house death was a frequent visitor; as a result, the family of those days was normally an extended one. The extension was not, as in the modern meaning of the word, a vertical extension to include more than two generations, but a horizontal one, gathering children of a single generation who were related to one, but not both, of the spouses of the marriage now in being.

In the Virginia into which Daniel Parke was born, a family composed of a father, a mother, and their children that lasted until the offspring married was unusual. Circumstances deprived as many as one child in five of at least one parent before the child reached fourteen; and by eighteen close to a third of all children were at least half-orphans, living in houses that were communities in miniature.

Because of the shortage of women in the early decades of the colony, the maternal survivor of a marriage was almost certain to remarry, as did Daniel Parke's mother, Rebecca. And it was a rare surviving father who made no effort to find a new wife to take care of the household, where her energies were likely to be divided between his children, her children, and theirs.

Thomas Ludwell, the senior member of that family, never married, but his brother Philip did, and the men and women to whom Parke was related through his marriage to Philip's granddaughter had nearly all mourned original spouses but acquired others as time went on.

Parke's own case was exceptional. Christopher Knipe, Parke's mother's child by her first marriage, did not live with the Parkes; he may have been raised by his father's kin, or he may have been old enough to be apprenticed or to pursue plans of his own by the time of Rebecca's second marriage. The transfer to him in 1655 of the 412 acres on York River that his father bought in 1652 supports such a possibility. He could also have been absorbed into the interests of his relative, Sir John Zouch of Derbyshire, kin to the Baltimores, who had become an advocate of western colonization as a member of the original Virginia Company.

In February 1658 the court recorded a deed of gift* from Knipe's new stepfather consisting of livestock and household furnishings that used to belong to Rebecca.[1] The goods included a new featherbed, bolster and pillow, and four cattle: the black cow, two yearling heifers, and a cow that must have been the family favorite, for while all the animals are described, this one's name, "Caull," was additionally recorded.

The three sisters of Parke's own family who went to England

---

*This gift was considerably larger than the single cow then commonly held to be an acceptable dowry for a daughter.

Philip Ludwell II (1667–?), by unknown artist.—*Photo, Virginia State Library and Archives; permission to print, from the Robert E. Lee Memorial Association, Stratford Hall Plantation*

when his mother moved home had been absorbed into the Evelyn clan and remained there. So when the senior Parke died in 1679 Parke's new position as an orphan also resembled that of an only child.

The family into which he married was much more typical in its structure, even if it was exceptional in respect to its members' official eminence. Philip Ludwell II, Jane's father, married twice. His first wife, Jane's mother, was the daughter of Capt. Robert Higginson, Indian fighter, and, when Daniel Parke, Sr., first came into the colony, military commander of Middle Plantation. A famous beauty, and thrice wedded, Lucy Higginson was a niece of Francis, Lord Cottington, Charles I's minister in various high domestic posts and his diplomat in several Spanish negotiations. The father of her first husband had contributed to Virginia's gubernatorial tree: Major Lewis Burwell, Sr., was acting governor (in the absence of a Cromwellian appointee) at the opening of the English Civil War; and his son's first wife was the niece of Nathaniel Bacon, president of the Governor's Council and thus acting governor of the colony. Lucy's second marriage was to Col. William Bernard who, though not a governor, had been a councillor and a colonel.

After Lucy's death, Philip married Frances Culpeper, child of one of the Carolina Lords Proprietors and niece of Thomas, Lord Culpeper, Virginia's governor in the early 1680s. Her first husband, Samuel Stevens of Boldrup in Warwick River County, was the son of Richard Stevens, the second governor of the northern area of Carolina. (When, as a widow, his mother became the wife of the contentious Virginia governor, Sir John Harvey, Samuel found himself simultaneously the governor's stepson and one of the planters whose opposition to Harvey ended in their "thrusting him out.")*

Frances's second marriage, to sixty-four-year-old Governor Sir William Berkeley, was cut short by his death in London in 1677. In

---

*Before being thrust out of office, Harvey swung a cudgel that thrust out some of his son-in-law's front teeth.

1680 Frances married Philip Ludwell II, owner of Richneck, near Middle Plantation. The marriage made him master of Greenspring.

Philip joined the line of chief executives when the Lords Proprietors of Carolina selected him as governor of Albemarle, "that part of our province . . . that lyes North and East of Cape Feare," which eventually became the separate colony of North Carolina. In 1691 the Lords of Trade in England enlarged his title to include all of Carolina. He handled his post as would a royal appointee, remaining in Virginia and designating lieutenant governors to act for him in Albemarle.

In addition to an illustrious genealogy, young Parke's Ludwell connection afforded him a voyage to England. In 1690 his father-in-law took him along when sent by the Assembly to present its grievances against Virginia's current governor, Francis, Lord Howard of Effingham.

Ludwell himself was at issue in this dispute. Appointed a Council member in March 1674/5, he had clashed with Herbert Jeffries,* expressing the view that Jeffries "was not worth a groat in England, and that if every pitiful little fellow with a periwig that came in Governor of this country had the liberty to make the laws as he had done, his children nor no man's else could be safe in the title or estate left them."[2]

The outraged governor thereupon suspended him from the Council, and the next spring the Lords of Trade ordered him excluded from it. But by that time, Thomas, Lord Culpeper, had been named Virginia's royal governor, and Ludwell had married Culpeper's niece, Lady Frances Berkeley. So, fortified by a unanimous request from the Council, Culpeper restored Ludwell to that body in good standing in the place left vacant by the death of Daniel Parke, Sr.

The good standing was brief. By 1683, Culpeper's successor, Francis, Lord Howard of Effingham, had arrived and raised hack-

---

*Jeffries was one of the Cromwellian commissioners whom King Charles named lieutenant governor on recalling Berkeley in 1677.

les in the community. In line with London's ministerial policy of royalizing the colonies, he put through an order for the burgesses, in their twice yearly sessions in Jamestown, to cease to sit as a court of appeals. Thereafter, a plaintiff or defendant disappointed with a verdict in his county might have to choose between taking his grievance across the Atlantic or accepting the ruling of the court of first instance. The governor next attempted to transfer the overall power to tax from the elected Assembly to the Governor-in-Council. The burgesses successfully resisted this order, declaring that "they can noe waies concede to or comply with that proposition, without apparent and signal violation of ye great trust with them reposed."[3]

The Governor then sought to enhance the Crown's income by introducing a new tax, a fee for affixing the essential official seal to deeds for land. The leader of the successful opposition to the tax was Ludwell. Effingham put him out of the Council again, and Whitehall agreed.

But the contest was not over. Ludwell's supporters in James City County took advantage of the spring election for the Assembly of 1688 to choose him as one of their burgesses. Effingham countered by citing a clause in his instructions that disqualified an excluded councillor from serving in the lower house and ordered a writ for a new election in James City. In response, Ludwell saw to it that his son-in-law was elected to the vacant seat, and for the two weeks in April and May 1688 before the Governor dissolved the Assembly, Parke was a member.

Then the Assembly decided to send Ludwell to London to protest the Governor's actions before the Lords of Trade, and he invited Parke to accompany him. Before sailing, Parke, on August 9, 1690, signed a power of attorney to be effective during his absence; under it discretion was to be divided between his wife, Jane, and his uncle on his mother's side, Major Lewis Burwell, Jr. (The Burwell and the Parke plantations faced each other across the York River; the young Burwells were of an age with Jane, and going and coming was frequent.)

The representatives arrived in London soon after the new English sovereigns, William III and Mary II, came to the throne. In the general atmosphere of amnesty that then prevailed, Ludwell's presentation, though it represented one of the earliest of the forthcoming transatlantic confrontations over tax matters, was well received. Though continuing to enjoy the title, Effingham ceased to function as Virginia's governor and was ordered to remain in England. In 1691, when Ludwell and Parke reached home, the House of Burgesses voted Ludwell public thanks and an honorarium of £250 for his accomplishments.

While the London negotiations were proceeding, Parke had had ample opportunity to view the way of life prevalent in such exalted quarters as Whitehall, St. James's, and Hampton Court. Since all government appointments were made in the name of the king, access to influence was purveyed from corridor to corridor, in both public offices and private palace apartments, twenty-four hours a day. It was understood by buyers and sellers that every position had its price; traffickers in influence and persons currently in office, having paid their way up, saw no reason why aspirants should not do likewise. Self-aggrandizement was a fine art, profitably practiced, and entrepreneurs of access who moved with a deft touch found their enterprise both lucrative and amusing.

Court circles contained influence purveyors of both sexes. Noblewomen who were mistresses of royalty or of royalty's favorites were among the best located; they were frequently longer tenured than the succession of ministers whom they advanced. During the early Restoration years when she was also producing an annual series of royal bastards, Barbara Villiers, the mistress of Charles II (successively titled Countess of Castlemaine and Duchess of Cleveland), was a very reliable avenue of preferment.* Concurrently, Arabella, the older sister of the handsome young officer John Churchill, future

---

*In 1668, popular gossip fathered on her yet another offspring, said to be by the then-unmarried John Churchill.

Duke of Marlborough, was delivered of four children while the mistress of Charles's brother, James, Duke of York. At the time of the marriage of James's legitimate elder daughter, Princess Mary, to Prince William of Orange, another Villiers, Elizabeth, who went to Holland as maid of honor to the bride, became the mistress of the bridegroom; but after the royal pair moved to London as England's sovereigns, William terminated the relationship. Her compensation took the form of marriage to the Scottish Lord George Hamilton; for Hamilton it was the award of the additional title, Earl of Orkney. Under that name, he was later a significant figure in the life of Daniel Parke.

James II participated fully in his brother's way of life; nonetheless, his production of two legitimate daughters secured the succession of the Stuart line for two reigns after he was deposed; Queen Mary II and Queen Anne were the children of his Protestant first wife, Lady Anne Hyde. Some London whisperers, however, questioned the parentage of the son officially attributed to James's second wife, the Catholic Mary of Modena. The boy was born in 1688, in the midst of the political crisis that preceded James's dethronement. John Evelyn's diary cites gossip of a newborn baby smuggled into the Queen's bed in a warming pan—the month was June, but Her Majesty had said she was chilly. James took the baby with him when he fled to France, where Louis XIV supplied him with a court of his own at St. Germain and, on James's death, declared the boy England's rightful king. But the English called James's son and grandson the Old and the New Pretender, and repelled the attempted invasions they both mounted during the eighteenth century.

At the day-to-day level of influence and placement peddling more likely to advance Parke's upward political climb, he could listen to tales of the prowess of William Blathwayt, the patronage dispenser who for his many petitioners produced amazing—if amazingly high-priced—results.

The results spoke for themselves in volume and elegance at Blathwayt's country house, Dyrham Park, in Gloucestershire, which was

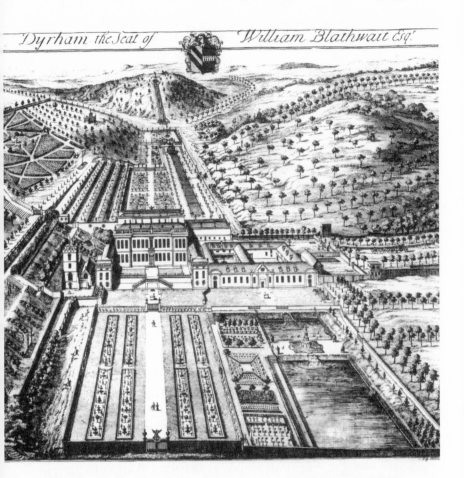

Dyrham Park, Gloucestershire (detail), the estate established by William Blathwayt (1649?–1717). Engraved by Johannes Kip (1653–1722), after drawings by Leonard Knyff (1650–1721).—*Colonial Williamsburg Foundation*

built between 1693 and 1698. The owner spread a wider net than most of the purveyors of patronage because he was willing to deal not only in cash, but in kind. His clients' cash donations for favors received paid the bills of the two great architects of the day who were designers of the east and the west facade of Dyrham Hall, as well as those of fashionable specialists in garden planning. Moreover, the Cordova leather that sheathed the walls of the room Blathwayt regarded as peculiarly his own came with him without customs inspection from a trip to the Continent, where his political efforts had been thoroughly satisfactory. But on another occasion the fine collection of Delft and other china he had assembled caught the eye of an observant customs inspector who, apparently not recognizing Blathwayt, declared that duty was due. The voyager's indignant outburst was promptly effective, but the shipment was somewhat delayed. More smoothly, teak wood arrived, compliments of the minister to Sweden, and marble and stone, thanks to the consuls in Italy.

Thomas Povey, Blathwayt's uncle, had been his initial sponsor and trainer. A courtier himself and holder of many positions, he occupied the first post established to oversee colonial affairs (with special attention to customs receipts). The governments of the West Indies and the American mainland remained his special interest. John Povey, Thomas's son and Blathwayt's brother-in-law, provided black walnut and pine from Virginia; and Edward Randolph deferred his naval activities—he was part pirate, part enforcer of the Navigation Acts—long enough to load ten tons of fragrant Carolina cedar on a ship bound for Bristol. The cedar wood was sufficient to frame a central staircase and to line the walls of two rooms. Today, Dyrham's magnificent gardens are gone, but the house, and these two rooms remain much as the original owner created them.

In terms of beneficial effect on national policy as well as on his private estate, Blathwayt's cumulative appointments served each other well, as illustrated by a Virginia example. In the mid-1670s, he became secretary of the Lords of Trade and Plantations and was in charge of their agenda. In 1678, he achieved a comparable relationship as clerk of the Privy Council. In 1680, he was named surveyor and auditor general of His Majesty's revenues in America. And in 1683, he topped his achievements by becoming a secretary at war. In each post, he left behind underlings with whom he subsequently kept in touch.

As auditor general, he ascertained from his representative in Virginia that Lord Culpeper had departed from his position as chief governor and captain general with £9,300 of the colony's money. As war secretary, he discovered that the departure had been without authorization by the King. Held under humiliating house arrest while these findings were coordinated, Culpeper never held office again.[4]

With the observations of English public life afforded him during this London interval, Parke returned to Virginia in 1692 with a program for his own gubernatorial ambitions well in hand.

Chapter 6

Up the Local Ladder

DURING the three years after Parke's return to Virginia in 1692 he moved amazingly rapidly up the ladder of public office until, by the end of 1695, he rested on the next-to-topmost rung. There, for two years, he enjoyed the perquisites of his positions, accumulating wealth to finance the last phase of his advance. Yet even though his political progress encountered no single instance of defeat, on a number of occasions his conduct caused considerable shock and disapproval in Virginia's Tidewater society.

The first instance of shock occurred immediately on his coming home from London: when he returned to Jane and their two small daughters, Frances and Lucy, born in the years before his departure, Parke did not come alone.

In London, keeping a mistress was a matter of no great comment, though on February 23, 1690, John Evelyn regretted that "The Impudence of both sex, being now become so greate & universal, Persons of all ranks, keeping their Courtesans so publickly, that the King had lately directed a Letter to the Bishops, to order their Cleargy to preach against that sin."[1]

In the colonies, however, even though slave concubinage was common on the great plantations, the maintenance of an acknowledged white mistress—particularly by a man with a legitimate family in the immediate small neighborhood—was unusual.

Parke's companion was soothingly introduced as his "Cousin

Brown," a widowed member of the Evelyn family whom Parke had befriended. (Sharper tongues identified her as Mrs. Barry, the unfaithful wife of a London captain.) In explanation to John Evelyn, Parke described his associate as a widow "Related to your fammoly . . . Acquainted with you, butt with ye Evelyns of Godstone verry well. . . . I shal allwaies be verry servisable to any that claim kindred to yr. famoly."[2] Not long after they reached Virginia, however, "Cousin Brown" clarified her relationship to Parke by giving birth to a baby boy. The father named him Julius Caesar.

Yet though tongues might wag, this liaison did not hinder Parke's public career. Within a year of his return, he once more occupied a seat in the House of Burgesses, where he had sat in 1688 after Philip Ludwell's election was disallowed. For the spring Assembly session of March 1693, the first under the new governor, Sir Edmund Andros, Parke was chosen to represent York County and given prestigious assignments. He was on the Committee on Privileges and Elections, and that on Grievances and Propositions; and he made a handsome, always modishly dressed leader of the official group designated to wait on the governor, or the Governor-in-Council, when there was occasion to present business on behalf of the lower house.

In the autumn election of 1693, he achieved a double victory, giving him a choice of two counties to represent. The day the House convened, John Custis, of the Committee on Privileges and Elections, reported that its review of the election returns indicated that Mr. Parke had been chosen by the voters of both York and James City and that he had decided to represent the latter. The double candidacy, based on his property holdings in each of the counties, was entirely in order, but a prominent citizen of Jamestown, William Sherwood, had protested the count. After a hearing, the House declared itself satisfied that the count had been correct; holding the James City election valid, it ordered writs for a new election in York to fill that vacancy.

Parke's occupancy of the James City seat solidified his position to the south of his home county. He broadened it again when, once more on eligibility due to property holding, he became burgess from New Kent, adjacent to York and farther up the peninsula, in the April session of 1695. For that session, he was named to the all-important Committee on the Apportionment of the Revenue.

In his own county, he resumed activities by again occupying the seat among the justices of the county court to which Governor Effingham had named him in 1688. His experience there repeated some of the court's agenda with which he had been familiar in his father's time. But some kinds of cases were newly prominent.

The legislatures of both Virginia and Maryland attempted to take compensatory measures when exceptional seasons caused gluts in the tobacco market, with a resulting depression of prices in London. Population increases constantly enlarged the acreage on which the plant was grown. One means of reducing the yield was to forbid the "tending of seconds," the harvesting of late-season leaves that sprouted after the normal harvest had been taken. Not only the additional quantity, but the lower quality of these seconds pushed down the price. Since policing shipments was difficult and costly, it was preferable to hold growers to a predetermined cut-off date for planting. The Assembly set the last date for transfer of tobacco seedlings from their starting beds into hills in the open field.

In 1687, Parke was charged with planting tobacco after the last day of June, prescribed by that year's Assembly as the final date for setting out plants. A jury was empaneled and heard two witnesses declare under oath that they had seen Parke's slaves breaking the law: "upon 18 July last past they did see the deft.'s negroes on his land and plantacon on Queens Creeke in the County aforesaid take plants up with their hows out of one hill and put them into other hills." Both Parke and his attorney William Sherwood pleaded that if they did, it was not with Parke's knowledge and was against his orders. The court found for Parke, but the informant, Thomas Dunkerton, declined to be satisfied with the verdict and announced that he would take the case to the General Court for review at its next sitting.[3]

Another action not frequently included in the court's minutes occurred on September 28, 1687, when the future manumission of one of Parke's slaves was recorded, with Jane Parke as witness. Virginia Will, the son of two Negroes belonging to Parke's father, because of his "true and faithful service," was to receive his freedom on Parke's death, together with "fifteen bushels of clean shelled corn & fifty pounds of dried beef to be as long as he shall live, also 1 kersey coat and britches and hat 2 pairs of shoes, two pairs of yarn stockings, two white or blue shirts, one pair of blue drawers, an ax, a hoe, all these to be delivered annually, and to pay his levies."[4]

A third exceptional court-witnessed arrangement was that between Parke and William Dyer, a wheelwright. Under Dyer's plan for working off a debt of £40, he provided security by mortgaging two lots that he owned; he also agreed to make thirty pairs of cartwheels for Parke and to serve as his wheelwright for a six-month period. The number of cartwheels—to be used on the two-wheeled carts in which settlers transported their corn and wheat to the flour mill—was an accurate indication of the state of the roads.[5]

Parke's success in the York County Court and the House of Burgesses was soon paralleled by his inclusion—"Cousin Brown" and Julius Caesar notwithstanding—in the body that took care of the affairs of his parish. Before going to England he had been a vestryman; indeed in March 1689 he had been one of the year's churchwardens, though his trip curtailed the service. He now resumed his former place. He also became a member of the Board of Visitors of Virginia's newly founded college, a position that slowly brought him in contact with a lasting adversary.

The Reverend James Blair was one of the Scotsmen recruited as Church of England priests in the colonies; his initial ministry was inland at Varina. Ever since his arrival in 1685 he had urged the establishment of a college where Virginia boys might receive higher education without going to England. In 1689 he was made the Bishop of London's commissary for the colony and soon received a living in James City County. In 1692 he undertook a transatlan-

The Rev. James Blair (1655/6–1743), Virginia commissary of the Bishop of London. Painted in London in 1703 by J. Hargreaves.—*The Joseph and Margaret Muscarelle Museum of Art, College of William and Mary; gift of Mrs. Mary M. Peachy*

tic voyage to put his case for a college before his bishop and the colonial authorities in London.

Spare of frame and square of jaw, fiery of temper and with a tongue that could flick a whiplash of disapproval, Blair was a perennial and formative figure in Virginia from his arrival in 1685 to his death in his eighty-eighth year in 1743. Since the presidency of the Governor's Council passed from member to member on the basis of seniority, his longevity gave him unprecedented control, and the

Companion portrait of Sarah Harrison Blair (c. 1670–1713), wife of the commissary, by the same artist at the same time. It was she whom Parke dragged from the Ludwell pew.—*The Joseph and Margaret Muscarelle Museum of Art, College of William and Mary; gift of Mrs. Mary M. Peachy*

decidedness of his views endured as long as he did. On the other hand, he took great delight in the social amenities of Williamsburg life. William Byrd II's diary records his frequent visits and entertainments at William and Mary's President's House,—from morning chocolate to late-day banquets,—even though the two men were frequently on opposite sides of questions debated in stormy sessions of the Council.

Blair had a knack of getting what he wanted; he could be a persuasive and persistent man. The college, called William and Mary, received its charter in 1693. The design of a building for the new institution soon arrived, possibly from the drawing board of Sir Christopher Wren, and further extended the turn toward brick for major public buildings. For it, as previously for Bruton church, the Parke brickyard was useful. The site of this imposing new addition to the town was the west end of Williamsburg's mile-long main thoroughfare, the Duke of Gloucester Street.*

While the new capitol was going up, the college building housed the colony's public offices and the Assembly met in its Great Hall. On completion, the capitol balanced the college edifice at the opposite end of the street.

While progressing upward in Virginia, Parke was also mindful of a lesson he had learned during his London stay: the average time required to achieve action in the colonies based on instructions from Whitehall was two years. Aware of this schedule, he had begun to accumulate recommendations for membership in the Governor's Council immediately after his return. In a letter of July 13, 1693, he wrote John Evelyn, the diarist, that if Evelyn would urge William Blathwayt to get him this appointment, he would give him a share in the profits of a distillery he had just set up. To the same end, he had already engaged locally in the manipulation of the governor, or, rather, in the manipulation of two governors in rapid succession.

While Parke was in London, and for a very brief time after his return, Col. Francis Nicholson was lieutenant governor of Virginia. Parke quickly undertook a campaign of blandishment, cultivating him to such an extent that Nicholson proposed him for immediate appointment as one of the colony's collectors of revenue, a lucrative post usually reserved for councilmen already in office. In 1692, however, Lord Howard of Effingham, who had been allowed to retain his title as captain general and chief governor of Virginia when

---

*The title used in naming the street was that of Princess Anne's little son and heir, her only child to live beyond babyhood, who died at age eleven on July 20, 1700, just after Williamsburg had been voted the new seat of Virginia's government.

the King confined him to residence in England, resigned his post. Nicholson was shifted to the lieutenant governorship of Maryland, and Sir Edmund Andros was appointed and promoted as a royal governor in Virginia. With a speed that was rather too conspicuous, Parke transferred his attentions to the new chief. Moreover, since Nicholson was a member of the William and Mary board, the transfer did not remove him wholly to Annapolis: he returned to Middle Plantation in connection with the affairs of the college, and the relationship between him and Parke lost its cordiality.

Sir Edmund embodied Parke's ideal of a governor. He behaved as one holding his title from the King in his own right should, and he exactly fitted the ministerial qualifications for colonial administration: he was a man with military experience capable of handling royal regiments in support of a consolidated imperial administration. He had previously served in the West Indies, and his first American appointment placed him in charge of the province of New York acquired from the Dutch at the end of the war of 1664–65. This assignment was soon followed by a special opportunity to carry out the policy for a closer-knit empire: he had been sent to the separately chartered colonies north of New York to take up their charters and bind them into a single whole, to be called New England and to be governed under instruction from Whitehall. Colonel Nicholson, also a man of military experience, was posted as number two under Andros, to take charge in New York when Andros went to Boston. The plan failed, disastrously. The New Englanders offered stubborn resistance. Violence erupted in New York. The two officers quarreled. Unification had to be abandoned.

Nicholson was transferred to Virginia as lieutenant governor, then moved to Maryland, with Andros taking his place in Virginia. The Maryland transfer came just when he had expected to be named Lord Effingham's successor; instead, he was pushed out of his gubernatorial chair and sent to Maryland to make way for his enemy. As Commissary Blair observed in a letter to London, Nicholson "was exceedingly angry that any one should be set over his head in Virginia, where he thought that his behaviour had earned him the government if it fell vacant, and especially Sir Edmund Andros, against whom he has a particular pique on account of some earlier dealings with him."[6]

The fact that Andros had had to be recalled from both of his previous American posts because of rejection by those he was sent to govern was irrelevant to Parke, who became Andros's devoted aide. In recognition of Parke's attachment, when Andros was informed that Parke's name had been inadvertently omitted from his initial list of council possibilities, he sent a special addendum to Mr. Blathwayt to assure that it would be added.[7]

While this was going on, Parke continued to appeal to John Evelyn for advocacy of his Council nomination. This time, instead of a direct approach, he sent a letter to Evelyn's son John, his friend from Long Ditton days, enclosing what John told his father was a "picture of your Cozen Parke and a gentlewoman very ill done." On October 6, 1692, John passed this on to his father with the comment, "I believe that you would easily prevail with Mr. Blathwayte when you are in town to adde my Cos. Parke to the Councile of Virginia, which is the request of his letter."[8] Three months later, in January, he followed this up with a reminder: "I have by a ship bound hence for Virginia written my Coz. Park, assuring him, you would endeavour to serve him with Mr. Blathwait, if possible to get him in one of the Council of that Colony, which I fancy he may do without difficulty at your request."[9]

By way of further pressure, Parke himself engaged the good offices of his sister Jane and her husband. Jane paid Sylva a visit, and Sampson Sherrard wrote Evelyn to ask if he would help, saying that Nicholson had recommended Parke to Blathwayt and "needs some one to second the nomination."[10] Sylva did more than merely speak to the great patronage dispenser: he wrote a strong letter of recommendation in which he affirmed that Parke, besides being the owner of one of the most considerable of all plantations in the colony, was as understanding, sober, industrious, and fortunate as any young gentleman he knew.[11]

Whether it was Evelyn or Andros who had exercised the greater influence on the appointment, on June 11, 1695, Parke took his seat as a member of the Governor's Council. Once installed, he obtained substantial appointments: in addition to continuing him as collector of revenue for the Lower James and combining that office with naval responsibilities, in December Andros gave him the lucrative post of escheator of lands. He also placed him at the head of the Virginia militia, causing him to be thereafter addressed as "Colonel."

Parke had arrived. With these extra perquisites, he had surpassed his father's life record. He had become one of the powerful and notable men of Virginia. Thinking ahead as always, he had already planned a campaign for achieving the final political preferment— the governorship. It could not be locally assured, but would require his presence in London. For the next two years, however, he would enjoy his perquisites, accumulate funds to be used in England, and relax the previous pressures of his timetable.

Two other factors may have been included in his calculations. A letter he wrote his Dublin cousin John in January 1694 mentioned the grounding of one of his ships, the *Loyal Evelyn*, the previous autumn, with loss of both ship and cargo. A stay in his current offices would give him the opportunity to recoup this loss as well as to enlarge the estate he would take with him.

He seems to have been living at Queen's Creek and perhaps desired a legitimate son. At any rate, the Parkes had another child at this time. The Bruton Parish register shows that a baby girl, Evelin, died on the twenty-third of November 1696.

During the 1695–1697 interval, Parke's day-to-day public behavior forecast some of the problems that would afflict his later life. He began to swagger, and he became a chief protagonist in a conspicuous public brouhaha whose other participants were Virginia's Governor Andros, Maryland's Governor Nicholson, and the Bishop of

London's commissary, James Blair, now rector of James City Parish.

Of necessity, because of their participation in various official capacities, these gentlemen were in frequent contact. All were highly vocal, and similarly prolific in the memoranda they sent to London or exchanged among friends. The governors wrote to the Lords of Trade and the secretaries of state; the commissary's sharply worded missives usually went to the Archbishop of Canterbury at his Lambeth Palace in London, though his correspondence was also familiar to government policymakers.

The castigations exchanged by these principals were often voiced in company; and when words came to blows, listeners frequently had to separate furious contestants. From time to time, bystanders put their own evaluation of the rights and wrongs of the quarrels on paper. William Byrd became so vigorous a supporter of Andros that in 1697, when he was in London and Blair was recalled for explanations, he was one of the parishioners to attend at Lambeth to present a point-by-point refutation of Blair's charges.

Each of the three top officials had his own grievances. In his private life Nicholson kept the community in lasting expectation of violence because of his unrequited devotion to a Burwell daughter. Major Lewis Burwell, the respected councilman, had nine daughters.* Nicholson had eyes for one only; after he had unsuccessfully, though repeatedly, demanded her in marriage, he threatened that if she married anyone else, he would shoot the bridegroom, the officiating clergyman, and the person who issued the license. But, although wedding guests may have held their breath, she married another in Gloucester County in a ceremony unpunctuated by pistol shots.

This private episode, in such a small community, was bound to have an effect on Nicholson's public life. One anthology of original documents includes a letter to the Maryland governor from a minis-

---

*Because of the Burwell marriage of Parke's grandmother, these were a part of his immediate cousinry.

ter telling him in no uncertain terms what is being said about him in London coffee-houses and on the Exchange. In ten numbered strictures, declared to be for his own good, this correspondent observes that

> it is here said by the meanest of those who have lately come in that you still prosecute your amours without the least hopes of success . . . and that you use such furious threatenings as to render you odious & hatefull to all . . . as your passions are very furious so they are very frequent that you are wont in them to swear & curse most horribly, & at best high vociferations are your ordinary language. . . . It is now in very many peoples mouths yt you are abandoned to lewdness, and some stick not to say to an instance thereof. . . . It is aggravated as a high scandal that Notwithstanding such dreadful habits of sin you are constant at prayers, which they cannot but think on the aforementioned accounts must be a sacrifice that is an abomination to the Lord.[12]

Yet even such corrections as these failed of effect. Later, when he had again become governor of Virginia, after the seat of Virginia's government had been moved from Jamestown to Williamsburg, Nicholson's office was in the William and Mary building while the capitol was under construction. It was said that, one evening, accosted in the hall by a suppliant who wanted to be given money out of public funds, "the Governor did fly into such a Rage and did curse and swear so loudly, that a Sea Captain, who lay asleep at some Distance in the Building, sprang from his Bed and, neglecting to affix his wooden Leg, came leaping through the Halls in his Shirt, thinking the Building to be afire."[13] The influence of such episodes on the scholars of the college was felt to be regrettable. One of the Indians was said to have expressed the view that the governor must have been "born drunk."

Yet the new college had no warmer supporter than Nicholson; his trips from Maryland to work with Commissary Blair on its affairs re-

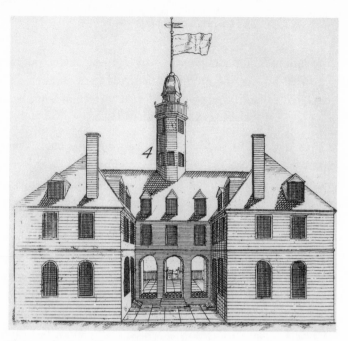

New capitol in Williamsburg. Detail from the "Bodley Plate."
—*Colonial Williamsburg Foundation*

Chief building of the College of William and Mary. Detail from the
"Bodley Plate."—*Colonial Williamsburg Foundation*

flected this interest. There were conflicting reports as to whether he did, or did not, observe the diplomatic niceties on these occasions; good form required a governor from another province, on entering the jurisdiction of a colleague, to announce his appearance in advance. Andros resented his prolonged presences and devised public opportunities to discomfit him.

Blair, an irascible debater in the Council, appreciated Nicholson's interest in his college and objected to what he regarded as Andros's inimical attitude toward it. He held Parke in contempt as a toady of Andros, and his cat's-paw; in briefing London he called him:

A handsome young man . . . who to all the other accomplishments that make a complete sparkish young gentleman, has added one upon which he definitely values himself, that is, a quick resentment of every the least thing that looks like an affront or injury. He has learned, they say, the art of fencing, and is as ready at giving a challenge, especially before company, as the greatest Hector in the town.[14]

Both the college board meetings and most Council sessions attended by both Blair and Parke became increasingly ruffled. After the spring Assembly of 1695, Andros took action to silence Blair's eruptions at the Council, somewhat inconsistently informing London that "All is very well and quiet here except Mr. Commissary Blair, who, notwithstanding all endeavors, was not to be satisfied; and his comport before the whole Council was such that they represented him as unfit to sit at that board. I therefore suspended him from the Council till further orders." [15]

Since the commissary's clerical gown protected him from the challenges to duel that Parke had indeed begun rather freely to offer around, the antagonism between them led Parke to take out his anger on Blair's wife. One Sunday in January 1695 the young hector created a horrifying scene in Bruton Parish church.

Following the custom in Virginia churches of the period, the box pews of Bruton's ground floor were paired on either side of the central aisle. Those in front accommodated the families of the ranking parishioners. Bruton's plan set aside two of these boxes for its most distinguished families, the Ludwells and the Pages.

Philip Ludwell II had invited Mrs. Blair, the former Sarah Harrison and his own wife's sister, to sit in the Ludwell pew.

As a Ludwell in-law, Parke had also enjoyed the privilege of occupancy in the 1680s; but after his return from England he tended to ignore the law requiring church attendance. It was thought that he took as a personal reference the frequency with which Bruton's rector since 1688, the Rev. Mr. Eburne, preached against adultery.

On this Sunday, however, he surprised the congregation by charging into the sanctuary after the service was in progress, storming his way to the Ludwell pew, seizing Mrs. Blair by the wrist, and dragging her out into the aisle.

The episode left those present "extremely scandalized at this ruffianly & profane action." The Governor-in-Council held a hearing on the incident, but finding themselves unable to justify Parke and yet unwilling to give satisfaction to Blair, its members avoided the issue on the ground that the matter "did not lie before them." And Philip Ludwell received a similar answer when he filed a complaint observing that Mrs. Blair was in his pew by his invitation. Even the Bruton vestry did not disqualify Parke from continued membership.

The Rev. Mr. Eburne promptly resigned. The 1696 vestry book minutes state only that "the said Mr. Saml. Eburne declaring his Intentions of leaving the Country, ye Churchwardens, therefore, are requested . . . to procure a Minister." But when the Lambeth Conference discussed Virginia affairs there was lively disagreement as to whether Mr. Eburne had resigned or been thrust out. Nothing was decided, and when the time came for his departure, the Bruton vestry, with all the insincerity normal on such occasions, subscribed to a glowing testimonial on which the name of Daniel Parke led all the rest:

We, the Vestry of Bruton Parish, in Virginia, whose names are underwritten, do certifie all whom it may concerne, that Mr.

Samuel Eburne, Minister of the said Parish, hath so well behaved himself in all his Ministeriall ffunctions amongst us for
the space of seven years and upwards, that we do all unani-
mously desire his further continuance with us; but, by reason
of his growing into years, he hath chosen to go into a warmer
climate.

Daniel Parke,	John Kendall,
Edmd. Jennings,	Hugh Norwell,
John Owens,	Philip Ludwell, Jr.
Robert Crawley,	John Dormar,
Henry Tyler,	Timo. Pinckethman.[16]
Wm. Pinkethman,	

But if Parke had had to strike at Blair through his wife, no clerical bar prevented him from unsheathing his sword against Governor Nicholson.[17] An armed confrontation nearly took place in the
commissary's house when the Maryland governor was there a few
months later. Parke accused Nicholson of showing around a letter
he had written him from New York. Those who had seen it could
detect no impropriety in its circulation, but the quarrel expanded as
Parke issued a challenge. The Council minutes of March 1, 1696,
record the efforts taken to counter the expressed intentions of both
parties to find ground on which they could break the law against
dueling without interference.

At the end of Parke's stay in the colony, his antagonism against
Blair broke out again. The Bishop of London, desiring to get a
firsthand account of the Virginia situation, had summoned his commissary and a delegation of prominent Virginians to meet with him
at Lambeth*; there the testimonial air was loud with the rasp of
verbal crossed swords.[18] The various contributions of materials for
the church were reviewed in minute detail: who gave a brick; who

*The conference took place on December 27, 1697. Those present, signified by initials,
were: C—Thomas, Ld Archbishop of Canterbury; L—Henry, Ld Bishop of London; P—
John Povey, customs official; M—Mr. Marshall; H—Mr. Harrison; Bl—Mr. Blair; and By—
Mr. Byrd.

Sir Edmund Andros (1637–1714), governor of Virginia 1692–1698, by unknown artist.—*Virginia Historical Society*

promised but did not deliver a brick; who restricted the bricks he gave to certain named parts of the church; who gave nary a brick at all. The circumstances of the Rev. Mr. Eburne's departure were equally closely canvassed:

H. M^r. Eburn, too, was turned out of Middle plantation by the Governor's own creatures, and this I have reason to know, for it is the parish where I myself live.

By. By what creatures? By Col. Park?

H. Yes; and by Colonel Jennings.

C. It must be a very pernicious thing. A minister will not know how to preach against any Vice, but some of the Great Men of his parish may fancy the Sermon was made against him, and so make a faction to turn out the Minister, though perhaps the sermon was made seven years before.

M. My Lord, I am confident if your Grace will but write to Sir Edmund Andros about these inductions he will take care to have that matter mended.

By. Indeed, my Lord, I dare say Sir Edmund Andros knows nothing of this right he has *jure devoluto,* or else he would not suffer the clergy to be so precarious.

Bl. I am sure I not only put him in mind of it, but gave it him under my hand and desired him to consult his Lawyers about it.

By. But, Sir, perhaps he thought not you Lawyer enough that he could depend on your opinion.[19]

Possibly because of the commissary's past record of securing the recall of governors, Parke had opposed Blair's attendance at Lambeth, saying that since the governor of Maryland was to be in London at the time, he could furnish the requested testimony. At a William and Mary board meeting, with all local partisans present, Nicholson denied that he was expecting to go. Parke insisted that Nicholson had promised to meet him there. At this, Nicholson declared: "It is a lie and it is not the first you have told." The governor was bareheaded; Parke, who had a horsewhip in his hand, slashed him across the head. The governor was also without his sword, having left it where he was staying in Jamestown, but he rushed furiously at Parke barefisted. The rest of the company pulled the two apart, and immediate damage was forestalled. Blair's narration of this scene declared that Nicholson had subsequently sent Parke a challenge to meet him in Carolina, the nearest place outside their two jurisdictions: "But Col. Parke for all his huffing and hectoring in company, was extremely nettled at all this, and contrived to have the matter discovered to Sir Edmund Andros, who by putting him under confinement, took care to keep his skin whole, but contrived no satisfaction for the Governor of Maryland."[20]

Once again, the Council minutes show that body's eagerness to avoid controversy: "His Excellencys warrant dated yesterday for confinement of Coll Daniel Park for breaking his confinement being read it is ye opinion of the Council that no application being made nothing further ought to be done therein."[21]

The potential mayhem terminated only with Parke's departure and Andros's recall. The governor's 1696 list of Council membership had noted that Henry Hartwell is "removed to England," and that James Blair and Daniel Parke are "intending for England." By the following April both intentions were being carried out. At the March court, Parke had appointed Jane his attorney with power to act in his absence, though she was not to sell or dispose of any of his lands, plantations, or Negroes without specific authorization from him.

The Council minutes for April 23, 1697, show that preparation of the official papers due to be dispatched to London with the spring fleet was in its final stages, though some signing had to be postponed for a day because "Mr. Commissary Blair was sent for thorugh the town but being gone out" could not be found. Parke was present.[22]

The minutes for the following day originally showed both Blair and Parke present, but a correction, made three months later at the request of Deputy Secretary Edmund Jennings, drew a line through the name of Parke. Apparently, and perhaps advisedly, Parke and Blair had decided to travel on separate ships; Parke's had sailed. In due course, both men reached London in safety, and when the Council met again in June, both names were missing from the register.

Other items also were missing. On December 14, 1699, the York County court heard a suit filed against Parke by the William and Mary board of visitors, who charged him with nonpayment of his subscription; after several continuances the court found him guilty and cast him to pay £25 sterling and costs.[23] Two years after his departure, the Council was still unable to recover the records that he had been obligated to send in when he resigned his posts as collector of customs and naval officer of James River Lower Naval District.

The final shock that Parke's behavior administered to the moral sensibilities of the community occurred at the very moment of his leaving, and balanced that which had accompanied his arrival. "Cousin Brown" sailed with him; but before quitting Queen's Creek, Parke handed over to his wife little Julius Caesar—thenceforth firmly referred to as his "godson"—telling her to bring him up along with their legitimate daughters.

∴

Chapter 7

Off to Parliament?

WHEN Parke reached England, he had first to answer two questions: Where would he live, and what occupation would bring him into the public eye as he pursued his coveted post as Virginia's governor?

The first question would have a double answer: a gentleman should have a good address in London, and also a country place. For the latter, Parke spent £4,400 on a property at Whitchurch, in Hampshire; from there he had ready access to town by the main road between Salisbury and London via Basingstoke. The only market town in the valley of the River Test, Whitchurch, was in an area of pleasant scenery, and from Parke's point of view it was competitively desirable. In the words of a later county historian: "In this part of the county there are no first rate mansions, but there are some neat chateaus, pleasantly situated; and the scenery is in many spots rich."[1]

The selection of a fitting section of London in which to locate took little reflection. London was still a collection of small settlements separated by green space. In one of these, the streets north and east of St. James's Palace, between Pall Mall and Piccadilly, were crowded the dwellings that housed the great and the would-be great. Above Piccadilly, streets named Dover, Albemarle, and Bond had been laid off, but the early version of Burlington House with its vast gardens resembled a country estate rather than a town house. Pall Mall was not a street, but an upper-class playing field for the French game of *palle maille,* a seventeenth-century pastime whose devotees attempted to drive a boxwood ball through a ring suspended at the end of an allée. The allée was part of an extensive garden below the backs of the houses that edged the south side of St. James's Square. East of this inhabited rectangle was the Green Park, and St. James's Park flanked the palace to the south and west.

The chief residents of the area were men and women who had appointments at the palace. At one time or another, all of the Stuart rulers had lived in St. James's; and Charles II, James II, and Anne had been both born and married there. Very recently the Princess Anne and her husband, Prince George of Denmark, had moved there from the Whitehall Cockpit after Mary II's unexpectedly early death brought Anne into new prominence as heir presumptive. It was there that Anne received word of William III's death and her accession.

Great lords such as the Duke of Ormond and the Duke of Leeds had mansions nearby. Great courtesans, such as Barbara Villiers, Duchess of Castelmaine and later of Cleveland; Hortensia, Duchess of Mazarine; and Arabella Churchill lived there. So did favorites from the theater: Moll Davis's property adjoined Madame Churchill's, and in Nell Gwynne's garden a mound enabled her to chat over the fence with King Charles as he strolled along Pall Mall. John Evelyn, on a walk with His Royal Highness in 1671, "both saw and heard a very familiar discourse between the King & *Mrs. Nellie,* as they cal'd an impudent Comedian, she looking out of her Garden on a Terrace at the top of the Wall, and [the King] standing on the greene Walke under it. I was heartily sorry at this scene: Thence the King walk'd to the Dutches of Cleaveland's, another Lady of Pleasure & curse of our nation."[2]

In this area, the numerous bachelor quarters were in high demand. It is not surprising, therefore, that Parke's first letters home were dated from St. James's. Addressed to his elder daughter Fanny, the first surviving letter, written just after his arrival, consists chiefly of standard parental admonitions, together with an indication that he has looked up his Evelyn sisters and that "Cousin Brown" continues to be part of his household:

St. James' October ye 20th

1697

My Dear Fanny—

I Rec'd yr first letter, and be shure you be as good as yr word and mind yr writing and everything else you have learnt; and doe not learn to Romp, but behave yrselfe soberly and like A Gentlewoman. Mind Reading; and carry yrself so yt Everyboddy may Respect you. Be Calm and Obligeing to all the servants, and when you speak doe it mildly Even to the poorest slave; if any of the Servants commit small faults yt are of no consequence, do you hide them. If you understand of any great faults they commit, acquaint yr mother, but doe not aggravate the fault. I am well, and have sent you everything you desired, and, please God I doe well, I shall see you ere long. Love yr sister and yr friends; be dutiful to yr mother. This with my blessing is from yr lo: father

Danl. Parke.

Give my Duty to yr Grandfather, and my love to yr Mother and Sister and serviss to all friends. My Cosen Brown gives you her serviss, and yr Aunts and Cousins their love.[3]

The second surviving letter was not written until 1702. This one brought news of his future plans and described his immediate past, but it makes no mention of his first, highly unsuccessful effort to gain prominence. At the election of late 1701, Parke had offered himself as a parliamentary candidate in the borough of Malmesbury in Wiltshire.

There was much to recommend this effort. During the five years he had spent in Virginia, the English political scene had changed markedly. When he departed, the transfer of loyalties after the deposition of James II had been incomplete. The former monarch's court at St. Germain in France was still receiving surreptitious correspondence from many Englishmen, who, though supporting the new regime of William and Mary, were keeping an anchor to windward lest it fail. By 1698 failure had become entirely unlikely.

Meanwhile, subtle changes were laying the foundation for a much more far-reaching development in the structure of English government than that of the recent transfer of the crown. Over the next decades, in the making of national policy, Parliament would become central in comparison to the prince. The doctrine that kings rule by divine right had been seriously eroded both by John Locke's general philosophy of a social contract between rulers and ruled, and by the specific stipulations of the 1689 Bill of Rights. The stark fact was that William and Mary held the English throne by Parliament's invitation. They were Stuarts, but Stuarts selected by an elected convention rather than by divinely sponsored inheritance, and a parliamentary Act of Succession was just about to designate who should come after them.

While the choice of political ministers (and their dismissal) remained with the sovereign, party loyalties in the country and in Parliament were growing stronger. Slowly, leaders were beginning to perceive the advantage of selecting royal advisors from the party that, at a given moment, held a majority in Parliament. Moreover, the rudiments of cabinet government were present, though as yet hardly recognized.

At the same time, because of a massive realignment in England's relations to the Continental powers, Parliament had been able to initiate new controls over the nation's financial affairs. While it granted more money to King William than it had provided for his predecessors, it also founded the Bank of England to manage the national credit; and the Bank was forbidden to extend credit to the Crown without parliamentary authorization. During the reigns of Charles II and James II, the Crown had been partially independent of home control by receipt of subsidies from the French king, sums of a magnitude that practically put England in the position of a client state. Now, however, Louis XIV's expansion across the Continent had begun to appear more threatening to the English than the recent trade rivalry with the Dutch. An anonymous pamphlet that appeared in 1701 warned:

> If both King and People do not concur in a speedy War against *France,* I am much mistaken in my Politicks, if we let *France* go on to heap Kingdom upon Kingdom, if we are not mistaken in our true Interest: The French King is grown a mighty *Nimrod,* a Land Pirate, that robs People of large Kingdoms; he's a Monopolizer of Kingdoms, and such a Monopoly is more dangerous than a Monopoly on Trade; for this invades the Rights of every body, and every body's hand ought to be against the Invader. . . . We must be in good ernest in the next War; Marching, Countermarching, and Intrenching will not do our business.[4]

On the spot in London, the far-reaching changes appeared as a series of responses to very present needs rather than as successive phases of a coherent plan; but to an observer who, like Parke, was able to profit from readings separated by a five-year gap, they could reveal the gradual emergence of a new center of power. A man who made a name for himself in Parliament now would be clearly visible to the sources of preferment. It was against this background that Parke decided to present himself as a candidate in the election of 1701.

To be successful, such an attempt required a powerful patron, a man who could effectively let his preference be known in the constituency where the candidate stood. Again through the family advocate, John Evelyn, Parke found such a patron in the person of Charles Mordaunt, third Earl of Peterborough. The Peterboroughs and the Evelyns had long been Surrey neighbors. The Peterboroughs had estates in the county at Ashstead, Reigate, and Fulham. Before John Mordaunt, baron Mordaunt of Reigate and Viscount Mordaunt of Avalon, died in 1675, leaving his twenty-year-old son Charles as his heir, he had persuaded John Evelyn to serve as the young man's trustee. Early in his career, the third earl lived at Ashstead and served as the county's lord lieutenant; his later residence was the Villa Carey, on Parson's Green in Fulham, a square brick house standing in twenty acres of fruit and flowers that were Evelyn's delight.

Charles Mordaunt's career was a bundle of inconsistencies. At Cambridge he had associated with the radical John Wildman and was active as an opponent of both king and church during the reigns of Charles and James. A legendary exchange between him and a Frenchman who was making inquiries about England's government reads:

> *The Prince de Cellamore:* Sacre-t'on les rois?
> *Peterborough:* Oui, Monsieur, on les sacre, et on les massacre.[5]

Yet Mordaunt is believed to have been the first to approach William of Orange about coming to England as king; he was present at William's landing at Torbay, and captured Exeter on his behalf. And as soon as William was in control, Mordaunt was inundated rather than showered with appointments: member of the Privy Council, gentleman of the bedchamber, colonel of a regiment, first lord of the treasury, Earl of Monmouth in the second creation of the title, lord lieutenant of Northamptonshire—and one of William's chief distributors of patronage. As such, Mordaunt offered posts to Locke and Newton; but others of the literati joined Swift in his estimate of him as "the ramblingest lying rogue on earth."

Yet Mordaunt's friendship with William did not last. It lapsed after he engaged in parliamentary actions the King could not countenance, especially proposals that a joint committee of the two houses review management of public affairs and his support of the 1693 bill that introduced triennial parliaments. In 1694 he was removed from the Privy Council and the bedchamber and had to assent to the transfer of his regiment to his brother. Rusticating at Parson's Green, Mordaunt began to interest himself in local candidacies for

Parliament. Various members of his family had been M.P.'s during the 1690s, and his eldest son—who had just come of age—had lately been returned for Chippenham in Wiltshire. Peterborough had also recently completed long-drawn-out negotiations for a major royal grant of an estate: Dauntsey House near Salisbury. At the Restoration, the place had reverted to the Crown following the posthumous attainder of its former owner; it had been used by the Duke of York for a time thereafter. Its acquisition introduced a Peterborough influence hitherto absent from that part of Wiltshire.

In contesting Malmesbury, Peterborough and his protégé were taking on a formidable opposition. Three powerful men were bent on buying up a series of constituencies to serve their parliamentary purposes: Thomas, Lord Wharton, future Marquis of Malmesbury, who had just served as the borough's high steward; Charles Montague of the Bank of England, newly created Baron Halifax; and Samuel Shepherd, wealthy London magnate who with his son Samuel, Jr., had just reorganized the East India Company. Malmesbury, Chippenham, and Wootton Bassett in Wiltshire, Newport and Andover in Hampshire, Ilchester in Somerset, and Bramber in Sussex were all on their list. The Malmesbury electorate of thirteen was composed of the alderman and the twelve capital burgesses. The scarcity of voters was reflected in the going price per vote, which might run as high as £1,000; along with many other constituencies, Malmesbury was perennially susceptible to corruption. In 1698 one of the active agents in Malmesbury politics, an attorney named William Adey, had openly announced that the man who gave him the most money should be the Parliament man for this borough.[6]

Adey was a former deputy steward of Thomas, Lord Wharton, a major Whig power both at Court and in the City. Like Mordaunt, he had been an early advocate of King William's assumption of the crown and he was author of the song "Lilli Bulero," which the Court danced to and sang when put to music by Purcell during the latter years of the King's reign.

Adey's defection from total loyalty to Wharton was fortified by the leverage he possessed over nine of the twelve capital burgesses of Malmesbury. In 1689 they had promised him, but so far not paid, £150 for his influence against a bill that contravened their interest in some formerly Jacobite lands in the area. Comparable activities had previously earned him a prison term in the Fleet Street jail and an exceptionally heavy fine, but his appetite had not diminished.

More discreetly than Adey's flat announcement, some of the notes that Halifax sent to Wharton during the last days of December suggest that other illicit practices were being vigorously forwarded. Halifax wrote that "there is something in this matter that must not be writ, & something not to be explained to you till the election is past, & yet they desire you should approve, if it ends well I think 'tis no great matter which way 'tis done."[7]

Parliament was in a difficult position. For a quarter of a century a flurry of anonymous pamphlets had cogently castigated the bribery and corruption all too regularly practiced in many rotten boroughs. Early in the Restoration, one of these had pilloried the men who

> love the king to such a degree that they worship his image; but then it must be upon his coin; their idolatry goes no further . . . if a little money will turn these mastiffs into spaniels is it not well bestowed? Therefore these gentlemen must be repre-sented to the king, as well-meriting men that have not had due recompense.[8]

The Parliament of 1695–1698, in a body, had expressed concern about the extent of abuses, and Lord Shaftesbury, one of its most articulate Whig members, was assumed to be the man who com-missioned a privately printed discourse on the proper purposes of a parliamentary body: to provide a balance between ruler and ruled; to advise the sovereign on laws that are necessary and laws that have become obsolete; to find the king's requirements for the expenses of domestic government and the cost of necessary wars; and to inspect "the public accounts, to know if their money is being applied to its true use and purposes; in short, to the best security imaginable to his majesty's honour and royal dignities and his subjects' liberties, estates, and lives."

Under such pressure, the Parliament elected in 1701 felt constrained to scrutinize the selection of its members rather more carefully than usual, strong-stomached though many were with regard to electoral irregularities, including their own. So as soon as the new House met in January, the Elections and Privileges Committee brought in twenty-four cases for review, constituencies up and down the country from Pontefract in Yorkshire to Thetford in Norfolk to Newport on the Isle of Wight—and Malmesbury in Wiltshire.

The Journals of the House of Commons record rapid action: on the sixteenth of January 1701 the House ordered that "*Daniel Parke,* Esquire, & Mr. *Gould of Dauntsey,* Schoolmaster, do attend the House upon the Twenty-ninth Day of January instant, upon the Hearing of the Matter of the Petition touching the Election for the Borough of *Malmesbury,* at the Bar of the House."[9] Where Mr. Gould taught is uncertain. He may have been employed in the Peterborough establishment at Dauntsey, yet on the other hand, in Tudor times, when the Dauntseys lived at Dauntsey House, one of the family who had become a City man had founded Dauntsey's School for poor boys at West Lavington near Westbury in Wiltshire and endowed a schoolmaster. However, this school, which still flourishes, has no record of a Mr. Gould.

At the same time, a petition was filed by a number of burgesses on behalf of themselves and others, charging that William Adey, a local attorney, and several accomplices had procured by unlawful means the election of Sir Charles Hedges and Edward Pauncefort to Parliament as representatives of the borough of Malmesbury.

The *Journals* of the House show the legislative day of January 29 to have been a long one.[10] The margin of one copy of its printed minutes carries alongside its opening an ominous handwritten note: "Malmesbury Election—a person delivers a Sum of Money." The accompanying text states that when the session opened Mr. William Adey was at the door, with a bag of cash and a bank bill that he said had been given him in connection with the recent election.

Map of the northern part of Hampshire, showing Whitchurch on north bank of River Test. Here Parke bought a country property on arrival in England. Detail from John Speed's map of the county in his *Theatre of the Empire of Great Britaine* (1611).—*Folger Shakespeare Library*

St. James's Palace, London. Engraving by Robert Wilkinson, in *Londina Illustrata*, London, 1819–1825. Parke's lodgings were in this neighborhood. —*Folger Shakespeare Library*

Called to the bar, he delivered a quantity of gold coins and a £200 bank bill and stated that he had received them from Daniel Parke for use in the election. As soon as he had given this testimony, he withdrew and disappeared. As an old hand in backroom politics who had been in trouble previously, he had probably thought it wise to preempt charges against him by virtuously turning in the proffered money at the very start of the inquiry.

But the House persisted in its investigation and by March had brought its resolution declaring that the Shepherds, father and son, had been guilty of corruption at every one of the constituencies on their list. Both of them, though immediate past incumbent M.P.'s, were expelled from the House, and a number of their agents were committed to prison. For Mr. Adey, however, his ploy on February 29 opened an escape: he was among those charged, but not located; on March 25 "the serjeant acquainted the house . . . That his messengers had been at Mr. Adey's house and searched for him and were informed that the said Mr. Adey had not been at home for 10 days" and had left no word as to where he was. The House thereupon resolved to ask the King to offer a reward for his apprehension.

As soon as it had finished all that could be done about Adey on January 29, the House turned to its main business of the day. It declared that Sir Charles Hedges, Knight, * and Edward Pauncefort, Esquire,** were duly elected to serve the Borough of Malmesbury, in the present Parliament, and dismissed as scandalous, false, and vexatious the petition filed by the burgesses and inhabitants who alleged corrupt practices; five of the petitioners were taken into custody by the sergeant at arms.

Next came a hearing on a proper use for the £300 Adey had brought in. Counsel were called to hear the charge that Parke had intended it applied to distort the vote by bribery; witnesses against and for him presented their respective views.

---

*Sir Charles was a member of a Wiltshire family, a Tory whom the burgesses had named the borough's high steward; through Godolphin, he was serving that same year as one of the secretaries of state.

**Pauncefort, also a Tory, was already an incumbent M.P.

By the time that counsel withdrew, the winter day must have been closing in; the next order is for candles to be brought. With their light came the finding:

> *Ordered* that *Daniel Parke,* Esquire is guilty of notorious Bribery and Corruption, in endeavouring to procure himself elected a Burgess in this present Parliament, that he be, for his said Crime, taken into Custody of the Sergeant at Arms attending this House, and that Mr. Attorney General do prosecute the said *Daniel Parke,* Esquire for his said Crime.

A similar resolution and order was directed against the schoolmaster.

This hearing is reported in the parliamentary diary of an M.P. from another area, Sir Richard Corks, and, though frequently illegible, it provides a running account of how a member from another constituency viewed the Malmesbury investigation.* The defense offered by Parke's counsel, according to this observer, took the line that he would admit Parke's giving the money to Adey, but would prove that his intention had been to prove Adey's guilt. Parke claimed that he had told Adey on the day of the gift that he was withdrawing his own candidacy. Counsel emphasized Parke's position as a man of quality, who could readily afford the loss of £300 in order to expose Adey's manipulation of the election.

However, a witness for Adey declared that he had hidden behind the wainscoat and overheard the making of the bargain by Parke and Adey. He testified that Adey had denied he would support Parke, who threatened Adey, demanded his money back, and "a great [dea]le more such roguery and stuff was said and proved." [11]

The House next took up a delicate constitutional question. Members were informed that the Earl of Peterborough desired to be admitted and heard. The propriety of a member of the House of Lords appearing in the House of Commons was questioned, but a

---

*I am indebted to the historian of Parliament, David Hayton, for a transcription of Sir Richard's observations.

resolution to admit him passed. In a dramatic entrance, "the Door being opened, his Lordship came in; and came up to the Bar: where a Chair was set for him a little within the Bar, on the Left-hand as he came up; whereupon his Lordship reposed himself a little while, covered; and then stood up uncovered; and was heard."

As soon as Peterborough departed, his supporters made an effort to close off further debate, but a motion to adjourn lost by a vote of 76 to 156. A question was then proposed: "That it appears to this House, that Charles, Earl of *Peterborough* is guilty of many indirect Practices, in endeavouring to procure *Daniel Parke* Esquire to be elected a Burgess." This invited a second motion to adjourn and it too lost, this time by 44 to 158.

The Peterborough partisans could no longer prevent other members from putting the main question: "That it appears to this House that *Charles,* Earl of *Peterborough* is guilty of many indirect Practices, in endeavouring to procure Daniel *Parke* Esquire to be elected a Burgess." The House passed the tellers for the third time, and the previous results were reversed: this time, the yeas numbered 141 and the nays only 56. The finding was then resolved in the affirmative, and the weary members, by coach, sedan chair, or the light of a torchboy, went home through the enveloping dark.

On February 13, the House generalized the Malmesbury decision by two unanimous resolutions: "That no Peer of this Realm hath any Right to give his Vote for any Member to serve in Parliament," and "that in case it shall appear, any Person hath procured himself to be elected, or returned, as a Member of this House, or endeavoured so to be, by Bribery, or any other corrupt Practises, this House will proceed with the utmost Severity, against such Persons."*

A month after the hearings, on February 26, another entry dis-

---

*Although the appearance of Peterborough, a member of the House of Lords, to give testimony in a matter before the House of Commons had raised very considerable objection, his loss of influence in Malmesbury was temporary. He had his revenge in the very next election, at which, in spite of the repetition of charges of corruption, his second son, Henry, was successfully returned for Malmesbury in 1705. By then, however, the father was far away, as co-commander of the English forces in Spain, where that year they obtained the surrender of Barcelona.

plays a further order related to Parke: "That the Money, and Bank Bill, which were delivered to the House by Mr. *Ayde,* upon the Hearing of the Matter touching the Election for the Borough of *Malmesbury,* in the county of *Wiltshire,* be re-delivered to the Clerk, in order to be made use of upon the Prosecution directed to be against Colonel Parks."[12] Here, without further explanation, the record ends.

Perhaps the voluminous and unindexed records of the Court of King's Bench conceal an explanation of how Parke escaped punishment. One or two writers, without citing sources or circumstances, suggest that Thomas Herbert, eighth Earl of Pembroke, intervened. He might well have done so, for he was both a former lord lieutenant of Wiltshire, and the current president of the Privy Council. Although conclusive evidence is lacking, the case simply appears to have been quashed.

One small clue may suggest a reason for the stay of prosecution. On January 29, and previously, Parke is regularly described in the *House of Commons Journal* as *Daniel Parke, Esquire.* On February 26, however, he appears as *Colonel Parke.* How he spent the weeks between those two dates may be related to the change of strategy he describes in his second surviving letter to Fanny, written from St. James's early in 1702. If civilian prominence was not to be his, what about military glory? England's trial of strength with Louis XIV was about to take the form of declared war. In September 1701, England and its Dutch and other Continental partners had signed a treaty of alliance patiently constructed by the Duke of Marlborough's remarkable diplomatic skill. Might not electoral misdeeds be overlooked in the case of a volunteer going forth to war?

Parke's letter read in part:

St. James, 1702

My Dear Fanny:

I am going a volunteer under the Duke of Marlborough, to Flanders where I served also the last campaign with my Lord Arran, the Duke of Ormond's brother, and was in every action.

God knows if I may ever see you more, but if I do not, I shall take care to leave you and your sister in very happy circumstances. . . . Be kind and good natured to all of your servants. It is much better to have them love you than fear you. My heart is in Virginia, and the greatest pleasure I propose to myself is seeing you and your sister happy. That you may be ever so is the earnest desire of your affectionate father.

DANIEL PARKE

I got some reputation last summer which I hope I shall not lose this; I am promised the first old regiment that shall fall, being now a Colonel.[13]

Chapter 8

Options and Positions

EARLY-eighteenth-century military campaigns were spring-to-autumn affairs: they began when mud-soaked roads dried enough for the wheels of the great guns to be sucked forward; and they closed when wet and shivering armies settled down to disease and drill in foreign winter quarters, and navy ships turned home for shelter and repair. During the winter, commanders formulated strategies for the next season and wheedled men and money from princes and parliaments. Senior officers, and even many subordinates, went back to England; Parke was among those who did so. Over the next months, while Marlborough took a hard look at the whole map of northern Europe, Parke obtained a modest position where, in serving Marlborough's headquarters staff, he would nevertheless be at the center of the ensuing action.

Marlborough's wide-ranging overview became the basis of his decision as to how to forward the continuing political and military objective of England, Holland, and other states and principalities of northern Europe: to limit and then reduce the power of France.[1]

After replacing England's old enemy in the Spanish Netherlands, King Louis XIV had turned to diminishing the Holy Roman Empire centered in Vienna under Leopold I of Austria. Bavaria was the largest of the German states that formed the Imperial Diet and was located so as to separate Austria from the Empire's other northern members. Louis XIV had lured Leopold's heir, the Bavarian elector,

Maximilian Emanuel, to change loyalties and join his side, installing him in Antwerp as viceroy of the former Spanish Netherlands. This development was in itself a significant change in Europe's balance of power, but the Sun King and the elector had more in mind. The current Hapsburg hold on Austria was acknowledged to be shaky. In the late seventeenth century, the Turkish sultan, Suleiman the Magnificent, had brought his army all the way from Constantinople to overrun Hungary and knock at the very gates of Vienna, and on his withdrawal the Hungarians had mounted a formidable revolt, which was still in progress inside the Empire in the opening years of the War of the Spanish Succession. Louis saw an opportunity to force the Hapsburgs to yield leadership of the Empire to Maximilian Emanuel; if that could be done, there would no longer be a balance of power in Europe. Louis's will would be decisive everywhere on the Continent, and England would have to fall in line.

The scope of the forthcoming hostilities would be as broad as all Europe, but the nations aligning themselves against France were for the most part not considering the Continent as a whole. They were concentrating on their own sections of it. To many Englishmen, while naval actions were acceptable, sending troops onto the Continent was sheer adventurism. Men such as the Queen's uncle, Lord Rochester, president of the Privy Council, and Sir Edward Seymour, speaker of the House, were only the more extreme members of a fair-sized group that held this view. When they thought of the Continent, most of them were thinking of the nearby shores of the North Sea.

To the Dutch, recent French occupation and conquest had centered their attention on their former holdings in Flanders. For them, the proper place for Dutch troops was in the garrison towns, defending their own borders.

To many of the small principalities of central Europe, the earnings of their soldiers as mercenaries were important enough to justify a certain flexibility in respect to their disposition. But they too were likely to include in their terms of employment provisions for contiguous or nearby territorial gains; the elector of Brandenburg, for example, had used the Allies' current need for well-trained soldiers to obtain recognition as king of Prussia.

On the northeast section of the perimeter formerly containing France, the breakthrough that occurred when the elector of Bavaria transferred his allegiance to the French had given Louis XIV an opening for attack on the entire structure of the Holy Roman Empire. This area of the map was the preoccupation of the Austrian minister, Count Wratislaw, as he went from western European capital to capital. He found most statesmen inclined to treat Austria as a faraway country.

In northern Italy, Victor Amadeus of Savoy's recent transfer of allegiance from France to the Empire was beginning to look doubtful, and so was the adherence of other princes on the Italian peninsula. Many of these were closely tied to Spain, and Louis's success in seating his grandson on the Spanish throne had spread French control of Europe from the mouth of the Rhine to the Straits of Gibraltar, monitor of the entrance to the Mediterranean. Louis thus appeared to have a broad range of options, with favorable prospects attending each. In a masque performed before him at Versailles, all the rivers of Europe offered obeisance to the Seine.

The immediate cause of hostilities in Europe was discord among the powers over the succession to the Spanish throne, the result of a sequence of royal deaths that occurred close together but in unforeseen order during the years 1699–1703. Previously, there had been agreement that the Spanish crown, after the long-expected demise of the mentally and physically feeble Spanish sovereign, Charles II, should devolve on Joseph Ferdinand, a grandson of Emperor Leopold and at that time Bavaria's electoral prince. But in 1699 this prince died unexpectedly, a year before the moribund Charles; thereafter, opposing candidates were advanced by the two major contenders. Louis XIV promptly placed his grandson, Philip of Anjou, younger son of the French dauphin, in Spain as Philip V, while the protesting Emperor Leopold demanded the crown for his candidate, his son the Archduke Charles.

Louis had proffered the deposed James II of England an affluent refuge in France. When this king died in 1701, Louis declared James's teenaged son, James III, rightful king of England. And, to the fury of the London merchants, he coupled this affront to the English nation with a prohibition of all English trade with France and Spain.

The French king felt secure against English resistance to his actions because of the low ceiling Parliament had placed on the peacetime strength of the English army. And, after a fall from his horse removed William III as king of England in March 1703 and brought Princess Anne to the throne, Louis expected political confusion across the Channel. His expectations were incorrect; no public opposition disturbed Queen Anne's succession.

Such were the political complexities of the theater of war. Military novelties also introduced technological elements into the strategy and tactics of the fighting of that war. New types of armament had begun to offer barely recognized opportunities. In the English army, the pike had almost gone out of use; the early form of the bayonet, introduced as a fixture attached to the mouth of a gun, had been rapidly replaced by the ring bayonet, which slipped over the mouth of the gun and lay parallel to the barrel, equipping a marksman with a dual weapon; he could fire, or he could thrust. So armed, a line of infantry only three or four men deep, as contrasted with the standard six, could maintain a continuous volley or move forward shoulder to shoulder in a bayonet charge. Similar changes were affecting the placement of the cavalry. Now rarely using pistols, horsemen were trained to advance in a compact trot that at close range suddenly became a gallop; the shock of impact followed by the slash of swords was well able to turn an enemy's flank or drive in his center.

Thus disposed, and with the new weapons, use of troops in a war of broad engagement could replace the traditional reliance on fixed sieges; a single battle deploying all available effectives could decide a campaign, or even determine the outcome of a war. The Sun King's magnificent engineer, Sebastien Le Prestre de Vauban, had fixed the format of seventeenth-century warfare when he fortressed the strong points of France with his superb star-shaped defenses, imitated far and wide by lesser powers. The military generation of Louis's greatness had accumulated its victories by a warfare of siege and attrition directed against successive enemy strong points; and the generals of the nations opposing him had followed his example. But now a master plan became possible whose objective replaced the slow capture of a series of fixed points with broad-fronted engagements that demonstrated national superiority rather than the capacity to acquire a limited piece of geography.

For the first eight years of her reign, Anne's government drew its executive strength from two exceptionally skilled ministers: Marlborough, her diplomat-in-chief and general of the forces, and Godolphin, her lord high treasurer, a comparable diplomat in the conduct of domestic affairs. The two men, far above other ministers in the confidence of the Queen, were lifelong friends. John Churchill, Duke of Marlborough, with iron patience, negotiated the Treaty of Alliance and led its forces; Sidney, Earl of Godolphin, handled the difficult thoroughbreds in the ministries and political parties with the same skill he exhibited, to their greater pleasure, with his much-admired equine thoroughbreds at Newmarket.

The Queen had a curious entourage. Chronic ill health, caused in her early years by the many births and miscarriages that brought her no heir and in her later years by persistent dropsy, reduced the scale of her court and enhanced her intimacy with her immediate women companions. It gave her unprecedented political advisors: first, Sarah Jennings, the childhood playmate to whom Anne was for many years passionately devoted; and later, in the final years of her reign, the High Tory partisan, Abigail Hill, Mrs. Masham. Sarah, Anne's Keeper of the Privy Purse and Mistress of the Robes, had married John Churchill, on whom Queen Anne soon after her accession bestowed the title Duke of Marlborough. With Anne and her own husband, Prince George of Denmark, this pair formed an inseparable foursome. In 1703 Anne wrote Sarah: "We four must never part, till death mows us down with his impartial hand"; to obliterate the differences in their ranks when they exchanged letters, she proposed they should use the names "Mr. and Mrs. Morley" and "Mr. and Mrs. Freeman." (King William, with whom Anne had quarreled in the 1690s, was known to them as "Caliban.")

The odds that England—and Marlborough—faced at the outbreak of war were formidable. England's army had been reduced to little more than a corporal's guard; Louis's troops were everywhere. If the so-called Sun King could replace Anne with the princeling a majority of Englishmen referred to as "the Pretender," Louis would not only possess England in all but name, he might well replace the Church of England with the Church of Rome and force on the Protestants of all northern Europe the fate suffered by the Huguenots of France when he revoked the Edict of Nantes seventeen years before. Responding to the German Diet, Anne had recently announced that "Her majesty regards herself as the Chief of the Protestant interest."

In negotiating a treaty of alliance that would include enough troops to confront Louis, Marlborough's first requirement was to secure and maintain a firm working relationship with the Dutch. The leader of the Dutch United Provinces, the Grand Pensionary Antonius Heinsius, understood the overall military needs; but the Dutch people were very chary of allowing their armies out of their sight. Louis's occupation of their line of barrier fortresses had left their country openly vulnerable to further French advance. As a safeguard, the federal constitution of the United Provinces provided that two deputies accompany the commander of their army and hold veto power over his plans.

Then, since the immediate purpose of the war was to force Louis to withdraw his grandson from Spain in favor of Austria's Archduke Charles, serious account had to be taken of the counsel and requests of Leopold's plenipotentiary in the west, Count John Wenzel Wratislaw. Any alliance that could stop the French advance must include all of the powers that surrounded Louis. Austria was one of the major three, yet it was in no position to be a powerful participant. Prince

Lewis, the Margrave of Baden, commanded a considerable Imperial army in the west, but Bavaria's shift of allegiance from Leopold to Louis had fractured Imperial unity.

The Empire's greatest contribution to Marlborough's alliance, not realized until 1704, came in the person of Prince Eugene of Savoy. This officer had exhibited his power as a commander during the final Turkish threat to Vienna at Zenta; thereafter, as head of the Empire's war council, he had vigorously restructured the disorganized Austrian Army. In 1704, bringing a crack contingent with him, he arrived to fight along the Danube.

In addition to concluding agreements among the ranking powers, further troops and allegiances had to be accumulated from the smaller central European kingdoms and principalities. As members of the Empire, each of their leaders bargained tenaciously for additional territory and enlarged political recognition, or at least, for ample subsidies for his mercenaries.

Perhaps the most delicate of all early decisions at the Hague concerned the designation of the Alliance's commander-in-chief. It should not be forgotten that at this time Marlborough's reputation as a commander was still to make. Even after his European campaign of 1703, many observers, John Evelyn among them, were apt to write patronizing and derogatory comments about his sudden advancement by Queen Anne:

> Thus suddainly rising was taken notice of & displeased those who had him til now in greate esteeme: He is indeed a very handsom proper well spoken, & affable person, and supplys his want of acquired knowledge by keeping good Company: In the meane time Ambition & love of riches has no end.[*][2]

---

*The change in public attitude that occurred after Blenheim can be demonstrated from the same source; Evelyn's *Diary* for Feb. 9, 1705 (vol. V, p. 584) reads: "I went to waite on my L. Tressurer where was the Victorious Duke of Marlborow, who came to me & tooke me by the hand with extraordinary familiarity & Civility, as formerly he was used to doe without any alteration of his good nature. He had a most rich George in a Sardonix set with Diamonds of an inestimable Value: for the rest very plaine: I had not seene him in 2 yeares & believed he had forgotten me."

Leo Belgicus, cartoon map of Holland by Famianus Stada, from his *De Bello Belgico*, Rome, 1632.—*Bryn Mawr College Library*

Various Dutch generals had longer records of service than he, and the Prince Consort of his own country far outranked him. Specialists in protocol supported Prince Lewis, Margrave of Baden, commander of the Empire's forces on the Rhine, and suggested that he and Marlborough share the command, taking turns on alternate days. Marlborough's tact eventually enabled him to serve as commander-in-chief, but his was a de facto position, accepted by persons who might have balked at his formal assignment to the role.

By a patient process of accretion, as the Alliance took form, agreements were concluded on troop numbers, subsidies, supplies, and so on. But the war began without consensus on how it should be conducted. Most of those concerned placidly assumed that traditional practices would be followed. They would have been surprised, and two years later they were surprised, to discover that Marlborough had different ideas. He had looked at the map of Europe as a whole, and he had familiarized himself with the new tactics that recent developments in armament had suggested. As a result, he envisaged a new kind of battle, and believed that the victory it promised was of adequate scope to save the political structures of England and northern Europe.

Chapter 9

Parke's Participation

W HEN Parke disembarked in Holland, he entered a territory that was foreign to his previous experience. From his earlier stays in and around London, his years as a participant in Virginia's colonial government, and his opportunities to view court and capital through John Evelyn's perceptive eyes, he had had a basis for judging political change in England as Parliament overtook the power of the Crown. But his interests lay in Virginia, and in Jamestown and Williamsburg knowledge of international affairs was fragmentary. Its sole direct sources were the impressions of a few American sons who had rollicked their way around the Grand Tour, the occasional older colonist who had recently been abroad; the treasured letters and dated news sheets that came in with the ships, and the rare European visitor. Parke needed to learn fast.

He needed generally to become alert to recent military developments as well, especially the new cavalry tactics; for Lord Arran's regiment, to which he attached himself, was the Fifth Dragoon Guards.

His military status was evidently that of a volunteer. The postscript of his letter to Frances, "I am promised the first old regiment that shall fall, being now a Colonel," raises some serious questions of fact. His boast that he was to command one of the English army's historic bodies of fighting men was on a par with his conviction that he would one day be Virginia's chief governor. He not only was never offered such a military post, he was even ignored when Parliament raised the ceiling it had put on the peacetime establishment and suddenly expanded the army from 7,000 to 40,000 men. The new regiments created required many new officers at the outbreak of the war.

So much is certain. What is not absolutely certain, but seems relatively likely, is the nature of Parke's colonelcy. He had became a Virginia colonel in the late 1690s when Sir Edmund Andros gave him command of the colony's militia; but there is no English record to substantiate his telling Frances in 1702 that he was "now a colonel," with the suggestion that he had become a colonel of a different kind. It is true that English military records are not without gaps at this period. Nonetheless, if he had been newly appointed as a colonel, his subsequent record in a specific post would be available, whereas the only available official reference to him concerns a post that did not bring with it any commissioned rank.

Perhaps he parlayed his Virginia title into verbal acceptance by those who addressed him; this could account for the change in the *House of Commons Journals* between the entries of January 29 and February 26. He might even have received an unrecorded brevet. His friend, Thomas Handasyde, had started with a brevet in 1697 and been commissioned lieutenant colonel in Sir Henry Balasyse's foot regiment two years later; in 1701 he was again listed as a brevet with the rank of colonel, and in 1702 achieved a regular lieutenant colonelcy in one of the newly raised regiments of foot and marines.[1]

The one English military document in which Parke's name appears remains the list known as the Blenheim Roll, which covers the positions of the participants in the final battle of 1704. In the list of aides-de-camp he appears as a "colonel," but the position did not carry a commission.[2] Altogether, there seems ground to believe that Parke's statement at the opening, rather than the one at the close, of his 1702 letter to Frances is accurate and that the position he maintained throughout his participation in the war continued to be that of a volunteer. Yet over the winter of 1703–04 he acquired a place that assured his presence, day after day, in attendance on Marlborough and his top officers: he was No. 5 on the list of twenty-one men who were aides-de-camp at general headquarters.

Parke's whereabouts in the earlier phases of the war are known from a small number of fortunately timed letters he wrote to his friend Henry Davenant.* Davenant was Queen Anne's observer in Frankfurt-am-Main, where the rulers of the northern members of the Holy Roman Empire were crowned. Two letters are dated, respectively, from midsummer and early winter in 1703, and a third from the midsummer of 1704.

On July 20, 1703, Parke apologized to Davenant for his failure to write recently, saying he had held off in hope "that I might send you something perhaps more true and perticular than you would have had in the public news." The "perticulars" reported explain the gloom that was enveloping Marlborough. The first Allied undertaking had been to force French evacuation of positions forming a mortal threat to the Dutch. Louis's armies had previously neutralized the row of Dutch strong points known as the Barrier Fortresses; these stretched across Flanders and Brabant from Nieuport and Ostend and Oudenarde in the area drained by the River Scheldt, and Mons, Namur, and Maestricht along the River Meuse. More recently, the bishop of Liège and the archbishop of Cologne, along with Spanish Guelderland above them, had shifted their allegiance to Louis. Maestricht on the Meuse was the only town still in Dutch hands; Huy, Liège, Limburg had been absorbed southwest of this area, and north of Maestricht the entire line of Stevenswert–Ruremonde–Venloo along the Meuse, and Guelders and Rheinberg between the Meuse and the Rhine, were French occupied, as were the forts on the banks of the Rhine at Kaiserswerth and Bonn.

Within its limited objectives, the Allied campaign was successful. If Parke, in accordance with his letter to Fanny, participated in all or perhaps even some of the successive sieges and captures, he

---

*My thanks are owed to Andrew Prescott of the British Library Manuscripts Collection staff, who transcribed Parke's three letters to Henry Davenant.

saw the traditional pattern of war at its most effective. By winter, Kaiserswerth had been reduced, and the string of towns from Venloo south through Stevenswert had been recovered for the Dutch, and Maestricht was still held by them. The final action by which unrestrained and enthusiastic Irish contingents took the Chartreuse, the great fort at Liège that included all the niceties of defensive design that Vauban himself could have thought desirable, was the climax of what was generally hailed as a splendid season.

Parke's estimate to Davenant was more moderate:

> I expect no Action on this side this year wee had an Opertunety at Henness to have fallen uppon them when wee first came there we allso had an other Opertunety that day wee pass'd the Saar . . . but there was no parswading the Dutch to Attack they are like ratts if you surround them and leave them no way to escape (as the french did at Eckterin) then they will fight like Divells; . . . I went wth the Generalls to view the French Camp . . . very early next morning we marched to attack the enemy's Camp but found they were retired to their lines. . . . the Generalls tell me there will be nothing more done on this side; . . . we expect to march bak & perhapps take Huy & Limburg.[3]

Marlborough's ubiquitous Dutch guardians had vetoed two opportunities to fall upon large masses of French troops as they crossed open country directly in front of him. From hindsight, they themselves agreed that each of these occasions had carried a promise of victory. But they had not permitted him a battle, and he was convinced that a step-by-step war for specific geographic areas was inadequate to overcome the massive opposition confronting the Allies.

Parke returned to England in the autumn; his second letter to Davenant, written on November 11, 1703, is in a much more buoyant mood.

> I was wth my Ld at Duseldorf to meet the King of Spain & came over wth him where I found my friend yr father in a good

post in the Custome House, I supp'd with him at his House wth the whole family last Satturday, where wee drank y^r Health, I am glad he is so well wth my L^d . . . Everybody seams pleas'd wth ye Queen's speech & I believe ye House will be Unanimous as to the carying on the Warre wth Vigour. Had my Ld Marlborough had an Absolute command wee had made A Glorious Campagne.[4]

Parke was exhilarated by consorting with royalty as part of Marlborough's train to meet and escort to England the claimant for whose throne they fought. And he was eager to reassure Davenant with his English news: the country was well disposed to the war; the Queen's speech on the opening of Parliament had been well received; and the House appeared ready to fund its part in the Allied effort. Moreover, he had visited Davenant's father and had joined with the entire family in drinking the health of their absent son. The only negative comment in the letter was that closing observation on the past summer: "Had my Ld Marlborough had an absolute command wee had made a glorious campaigne."

The campaign of 1703 was in fact so great a disappointment to Marlborough that he seriously considered resigning his post. His current proposal to attack the French-occupied area sheltered behind the lines of Brabant (present-day Belgium) had been denied out of hand. Discord among the smaller allies began to threaten Alliance unity. Further east in Europe the situation was deteriorating as French forces joined up with forces the Elector had left in Bavaria. The Empire in Vienna staggered. The Dutch, much relieved by recent events, happily struck a medal for presentation to Marlborough, inscribed: "Victorious without slaughter, by the taking of Bonn, Huy and Limburg." But Marlborough was acutely aware that nothing much else had been accomplished. That was why, in planning the campaign of 1704, he determined, without risking further vetoes, to try a hitherto untried type of encounter.

As the fireside experts of 1703 gathered in the coffeehouses of London and the homes of leaders of English public life, forecasters of the campaign of 1704 prophesied a march up the Rhine and a thrust into France along one of the rivers. They were in error.

The exact sequence of what went on in Marlborough's mind is his secret. After a return to Holland in late January, he was importuned by Count Wratislaw to campaign along the Danube. A short time later he returned from another trip to England with authorizations from the Queen that included separation from the Dutch of the English army and the Continental allies in English pay. That separation at least gave him an independent command,—smaller, but free of vetoes. If his plan was to be attempted, it must be held absolutely secret until the last possible moment. At the opening of May he informed the Dutch that he was moving the troops under his sole command to Coblenz en route to the Moselle; but he wrote Godolphin that "When I come to Phillipsburg, if the French shall have joined any more troops to the Elector of Bavaria, I shall make no difficulty of marching to the Danube." Shortly thereafter, he held a grand review of his troops at Bedburg, north of Cologne, and set forth up the Rhine.

Daniel Parke had returned from England some two weeks previously; an official pass for a crossing from Harwich was issued for him (and three servants) on April 24.[5]

As the march of the Allied army continued, all Europe was puzzled. When Marlborough passed the mouth of the Moselle at Coblenz on May 28, it was clear that penetration of France along this watercourse was not the year's objective after all. When his infantry turned east from the Rhine below Heidelberg—the cavalry had already done so—it was obvious that he was not even going to attempt to enter France via Alsace. Day after day, the red line of marching men that Winston Churchill has called "the scarlet caterpiller" inched its way, at a rate of some ten to fifteen miles.

The state of the roads was lamentable. Their condition is a standard subject of the deeply religious diary of the Scottish Presbyterian, Col. John Blackader. His usual day's opening is "Army marching," but there were occasions when the troops could not march until road repairs had been made. As they approached Mainz, he wrote:

> Resting this day, not designedly, but by reason of the roads. I know not where they are leading me, but, Lord, do thou lead me in thy way. I will not trust to generals leading; thou who leadest the blind by the way they know not, I trust to thee alone, and put myself, and all I am concerned in, under thy conduct. I see the kind hand of a father still about me.[6]

Two weeks later, when the army was at rest in a welcome break, he enjoyed an opportunity for reflection sheltered by a rock:

> When the carcases of the one half of us are dung on the earth, in Germany, perhaps the other half will bethink themselves. But it as thou wilt, O Lord. I bless thee I have such sweet minutes in such an army; they are cordials which keep my fainting spirits. At the writing hereof, I am sitting (it is a scorching hot day) under a great rock, cool and refreshed; even so, Lord Jesus, be thou the shadow of a great rock in this weary land to me.[7]

On June 10 when the army had reached Mundelheim, an historic meeting took place. For the first time, Marlborough and Prince Eugene of Savoy saw each other face to face. Their exchange of views, continuing far into the night, began a comradeship that lasted throughout their lives and was unmarred by any trace of professional jealousy. In temperament as in appearance utterly different, they were in total accord on their concept of modern war.

Over the following days these two, with the Margrave of Baden and Ambassador Wratislaw usually joining them, laid their plans. Eugene, for the present, would command Allied forces in the west, holding the French army under Maréchal de Villeroi in place. The Margrave and Marlborough would continue the current Allied march east.

Once again, there was the question of the top command. By all

John Churchill, first Duke of Marlborough (1650–1722). Engraved by Johannes Houbraken in 1742, from portrait by Martin Maingaud.
—*Trustees of the British Library*

Prince Eugene of Savoy (1663–1736), Marlborough's boon companion and co-commander. Second frontispiece, *The Lives of the Two Illustrious Generals, John, Duke of Marlborough, and Francis Eugene, Prince of Savoy*, London, 1713. —*Library of Congress, Rare Book Room*

the considerations of protocol, in rank, years, and experience, the Margrave held precedence. But his concept of war was not the same as that of Eugene and Marlborough. Lewis was a practiced officer of the old school. He understood siege warfare, and conducted it well even if he combined his military capacities with a good deal of caution. Recently, however, in addition to his differences from the other two commanders over strategy, his conduct had created some doubts in respect to the fervor of his desire to damage territories belonging to the Elector of Bavaria. The awkwardness of a daily alternation of command had to be accepted for want of a better arrangement. But if Marlborough had freed himself from his Dutch naysayers, a half-command remained his daily portion.

On June 25 at Elchingen, Marlborough's forces turned sharply north, avoiding the major fortress at Ulm on the Danube where the French Maréchal Marsin and the Elector of Bavaria had stationed some 45,000 troops. Fifteen miles farther along the Danube was Donauwörth, where the River Wörnitz, flowing south from Nürnberg, joins the Danube at the foot of a formidable hill, the dome-shaped Schellenberg. Its top is only 900 feet above sea level, but for ages beyond history this steep rise had determined the fortunes of armed men. Most recently, from a fort at the top, King Gustavus Adolphus of Sweden had commanded the entire countryside, miles on miles of slightly rolling agricultural land stretching to the horizon, interspersed with woods, pointed up occasionally by the church spire of a prosperous village. Here was an obstacle that fighters trained in seventeenth-century warfare fully understood; the invaders had to take that strong point if they were to continue east and put Bavaria out of the war.

Chapter 10

The Storming of the Schellenberg

PARKE'S participation in the storming of the Schellenberg was not that of an aide; in concentrated fighting on a single hill, the voice communications of the commanders sufficed. In that battle, too, every fighting man was needed, and Parke changed roles.

The hill is on the eastern bank of the Wörnitz, and the top was then thickly forested.* The difficulties for troops attempting to reach the fortress on this height were formidable; artillery in the town of Donauwörth could loft cannonballs almost all the way to the edge of the forest. Only along a narrow strip of land below the trees could troops beat their way into the angled entrance of the fort above the persistent rain of stone and metal. The climb from ground level is fairly short, but the slopes were, and are, very steep and covered with slippery grasses by which the storming troops had to pull their way up, muskets slung across their backs or over their shoulders.

The French and Bavarian commanders at Ulm, monitoring Marlborough's passing and aware that he had to gain this summit if he were to carry hostilities farther, had dispatched the Piedmontese general, Count d'Arco, with men and materials to renew and extend the fort's defenses. Circling the top of the dome, the walls left considerable room for maneuver within their limits. Work was rushed

---

*For much help, and for all of the German illustrations in this and the following chapter, I am grateful to Dr. Lore Grohsmann, archivist of Donauwörth, Bavaria.

in frantic haste; its completion was set for the end of the day of July 2, N.S.* before which the French and Bavarians were convinced that Marlborough's main army could not arrive.

Their estimate was correct. The Allied troops appeared about 4 P.M., having marched since early morning. Only a few hours of daylight remained; but after inspecting the site Marlborough decided that he must act before the reinforcements expected by his enemy arrived. Using every available man, in the light of these remaining hours, he took the Schellenberg.

Only his uncanny sense of timing of when and where to strengthen a struggling line prevented a disaster that would have precluded farther advance. As his soldiers heaved their way up the slick slopes, inert bodies began to slide back. As forward units reached the walled angle of the fort entrance, bodies of dead and wounded began to clog the way. The first wave faltered—army slang gave the name of "the forlorn Hope" to the contingent sent to open a battle and attract the initial fire. Immediately Marlborough ordered a second wave. As it, too, faltered, he brought up additional squadrons in such close order as to prevent withdrawal.

About this time the Margrave began his attack, directing it to the right of the troops already involved. His charge became a break-through; the enemy forces there had been drawn off, and the Allied infantry poured through the gap to join with comrades who had successfully forced the contested entrance.

Simultaneously, Marlborough's third wave began to push the defenders inward, first across the dome and then out of the fort on the other side. Many ran down the southeastern face of the hill toward

---

*To correct the Roman calendar, which over the centuries had rendered the days and months of the year increasingly discordant with the seasons, in 1582 Pope Gregory introduced a new and more accurate version. Adopted by most of the Catholic nations, the Gregorian calendar was not accepted by England for another 169 years, in 1751. Until then, there was a difference of ten to eleven days between British and Gregorian dating, and dates were given as O.S. (Old Style) or N.S. (New Style). Thus the Battle of Blenheim, fought at the end of the midsummer of 1704, was listed in England as having taken place August 2 O.S., whereas the French used the Gregorian calendar's date of August 13 N.S. In this book, where relevant, dates have been made to correspond to the calendar of the country in which events occur.

Panorama of Donauwörth and the Schellenberg by Michael Wening (1645–1718), copperplate engraver. From *Historico-topographica descriptio*, Part I,

the French-built pontoon bridge leading to their camp across the river only to find it badly damaged by previous traffic. Once more on horseback, Allied cavalrymen, who had dismounted to aid the infantry at the fort, rode down many of those in flight and chased others into the roiling water. The day—it was now well on toward night—ended with the surrender of the town of Donauwörth.

Parke was in the midst of this. In a short letter to Henry Davenant on July 13, 1704 N.S. he describes his part in the Schellenberg fighting.[1] When the day's "forlorn Hope" opened the attack, its two officers, Blunt and West, were shot dead, and so were three of the four sergeants with them. Replacing the officers, Parke led the two

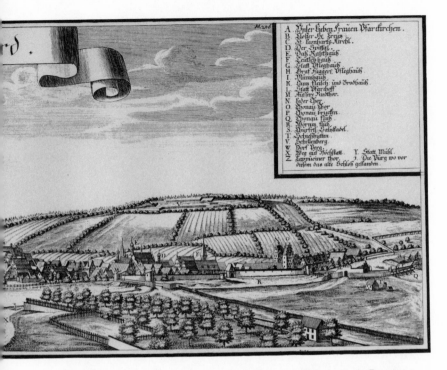

Munich, 1701.—*Graphics Collection, City Archives of Donauwörth, Bavaria*

remaining platoons. He was shot in both legs but not so seriously as to prevent him from remaining in the battle all day. (He is afraid however, that lack of care for the wound in his right leg may cause permanent injury as he has not been able to get proper treatment for a cyst on his ankle.)

Parke also informs Davenant that since the battle Marlborough's troops have been busy crossing the Danube and the Lech. They are presently held up by a small town, "a little foolish dyrt pie called Rain" defended by about 900 men.[2] There they were short of battering guns to break down the walls, and are still short of shot for them. At Ausburg, he reports, the enemy has entrenched himself so thoroughly that it cannot be taken; and Munich too has been secured by trenches. The night before, the enemy garrison had made a sally and gathered up the fascines (bundles of bush tied together) that the Allied forces had readied to fill up the ditches.

Deserters estimate the enemy strength at 50,000; the Allies put it closer to 30,000, believing that about 8,000 men had been killed, drowned, or captured on the Schellenberg. But the French are expecting generals Tallard and Villeroi to join them. They have evacuated Donauwörth and Nauberg, where Prince Lewis has set up an Allied garrison.

Parke finds Prince Lewis less than zealous in the cause, though on the Schellenberg he was at the head of his men when they made the charge that first broke the enemy. The Prince was wounded in the foot but is now up again, though not yet fully recovered.

Close to the center of Allied plans though he was, Parke seems to believe that the taking of the Schellenberg was the climax of the year's campaign: "I do think that in one fortnight more all will be done that can: I sopose wee shall eighther go^e to Ingollstadt or Munick after wee have taken this town." The letter closes with some personal plans reaffirming his conviction that the campaign is practically over. He says he is obliged to go to England and must be there by August 11 or 12. He plans to come to Frankfurt on his own horses and either sell them there or leave his man to follow at a more leisurely pace while he takes the post wagon. It seems possible that his planned trip to London may have involved financial problems, for in a postscript he returns to the horses—does Davenant know of a possible purchaser? He also has and will bring "a very pretty young hunting pack that cost me this year thirty Guineas in London."[3]

Parke's estimate of the French and Bavarian casualties at the Schellenberg is more or less in line with the figures given by the Allied forces. For the Allies the cost of victory had been close to prohibitive: casualties in those few afternoon hours had numbered some 5,500—1,400 of them dead. The hospitals Marlborough had

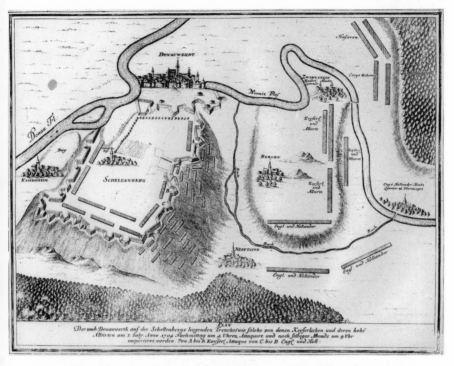

The Storming of the Schellenberg. Copperplate from *Chur-Baiern, Anderer Theil. Als eine jäh-veränderte Schaubühne*. Sold at Frankfurt and Leipzsig, 1704 by Christoph Riegeln.—*Graphics Collection, City Archives of Donauwörth, Bavaria*

The retreat of the French and Bavarian forces after the Allied victory at the Schellenberg on July 2, 1704. Copperplate by Jeremias Wolff after Georg Philipp Rugendas.—*Graphics Collection, City Archives of Donauwörth, Bavaria*

readied were overwhelmed. Throughout the night many wounded men, still uncleansed from the bloody escarpments, lay soaked in the rain. Total figures vary, but among senior officers included in the Allied dead or wounded were eleven lieutenant generals, four major generals, and twenty-eight brigadiers, colonels, and lieutenant colonels.

Joseph Addison's poem, *The Campaign* mourned the toll:

> How many generous Britons meet their doom,
> New to the field, and heroes in their bloom . . .
> After such toils o'ercome, such dangers past,
> Stretched on Bavarian ramparts breathe their last.

In the western European nations whose troops had been thus decimated, Marlborough was denounced. The Dutch again struck a medal, with the motto: "The enemy defeated and put to flight and their camp plundered at Schellenberg near Donauwörth." But this year they gave it to the Margrave.

Chapter 11

Glory in Abundance

ONCE in control of the Schellenberg, Marlborough, after moving somewhat farther east, spent the rest of July, day by day, putting into effect a policy of scorched earth on fields almost ready for harvest. He knew that the result would be to turn the Bavarian peasantry against the Elector, and his purpose was to put Bavaria out of the war.

Everywhere, men and soldiers accustomed to the niceties of past wars denounced the fires as barbarous. But though this was his own country, the Bavarian Elector attempted no defense. Day after day, the horizon was smudged by the smoke of burning farmsteads. Ingoldstadt might be the only fortress on the Danube between Ulm and Passau remaining in his control, but Maximilian Emanuel scattered his forces far and wide to protect individual properties, especially his own. So far, he had no mind to withdraw from the war. When the French commanders urged him to recall his forces to public use, he indicated that he would do so when the French succor he anticipated arrived. The general expectation was that Marlborough would soon take his armies home.

On both sides, the camps were under unusually divided commands. The ranking French general was a man Marlborough knew rather well: Camille d'Hostun, Duc de Tallard and maréchal de France, like Marlborough, was a diplomat as well as a military leader and had been Louis's representative at London until the spring of

1701. As the ranking general, he led the Sun King's eastern forces, which were gathered on the south bank of the Danube. But the Comte de Marsin, also a maréchal, and the Bavarian Elector shared control of the forces lying to Tallard's west. These three directed the army that, puzzled but persistent, had followed Marlborough as he descended the Danube. The Duc de Villeroi, a third maréchal, still held the French lines west of the Rhine.

Prior to the attack on the Schellenberg, the Allied forces in the east had served under the alternating command of Marlborough and the Margrave, the troops in the west under the Prince of Savoy. But after the attack, the Margrave and Marlborough took a risky decision to reduce the strength of the western defenses and chance a disaster there if Villeroi should open a new front. Eugene moved west to join forces with the army in Bavaria, and become a third commander.

The question in the minds of the French—and indeed of all of Europe—was, what will Marlborough do next? His taking of the Schellenberg had been a feat more than adequate to fulfill the requirements of a summer campaign; yet he was lingering and ravaging the countryside to an extent that would make it impossible for him to live off the country if he stayed into the winter. Why didn't he start home? Tallard resolved to trail him closely until his destination was clearly discernible.

Eugene arrived on August 6 N.S. with 18,000 men, and camped on the north bank of the river between Lauingen and Donauwörth; Marlborough was on the south bank, below Rain. The Margrave's proposal for their next move favored a traditional siege of Ingoldstadt, some thirty miles east of their present position, to clear the river all the way to the friendly borders of Austria. It was the kind of operation he understood, and he was eager to command it. His co-commanders were entirely willing that he should do so, even to the extent of furnishing forces beyond his estimate of what was necessary. He went forward to inspect preparations at once, returned to report on the seventh, and departed to invest the strong point the next day.

Late on August 10 N.S. Marlborough received a message from Eugene that Tallard and the Elector were crossing the river at Lauingen with their entire army; they then turned east toward the town of Höchstädt, arriving on the eleventh. Eugene moved to a position northwest of Donauwörth, and Marlborough crossed the river at Donningburg southeast of the town, while his brother, Lt. Gen. Charles Churchill, directed a crossing still farther east, at Merxheim. The French interpreted these movements as preliminaries to departure; unaware that a siege had been begun at Ingoldstadt, they assumed the Margrave to be with the others. Since there was no objective in the immediate area that invited military occupation, the French high command saw no reason to anticipate hostilities; on the night of the twelfth they dined well and slept well—only to be roused at 2:00 A.M. by sounds of their opponents preparing for immediate attack.

Eugene and Marlborough, riding together across the great fields along the river shore between Höchstädt and Blenheim, had concluded that the terrain would well serve the requirements of the far-flung, new-style battle both of them longed to fight.

Next day, pooling their skills, they fought it.

The encounter that began with the rousing of the camps lasted all day, with continuous action from midday until dusk. Both armies were now north of the Danube, but between them ran a broad brook, the Nebel, which was marshy at its edges. Each army faced the other in the positions its units had maintained on the march eastward. The right and center of the French line was commanded by the Maréchal Tallard, the left by the Maréchal Marsin, the far left by the Bavarian Elector. To anchor his right firmly on Blenheim, Tallard crowded some twenty-seven battalions and four regiments of dismounted dragoons into the village of Blenheim and onto the strip of land between it and the Danube. The juncture of the two French commands, and a concentration of their infantry, occurred at the area where slightly higher ground improved the possibility of troops crossing the Nebel.

The Allied right was under the command of Eugene, the left of Marlborough, with important German, Dutch, and Danish units attached to each. Marlborough's order of battle ranged his troops in an arc north of the Nebel between the towns of Unterglaub and Blenheim, with a heavy concentration of cavalry at the center.

The opening engagement of the battle was commanded by the Irish general, Lord Cutts; he had fought with King William at the Boyne and joined Marlborough at the beginning of the war on the Continent. After he had launched two unsuccessful attacks on Blenheim, Marlborough ordered him merely to hold his previous line.

Meanwhile, Marlborough had driven some of the French stationed farther west back across the Nebel and prepared a massive crossing of his own. When Eugene's parallel engagement with the Elector's army had achieved a difficult success, Marlborough, personally in the lead, took almost all of his troops, other than those confining Blenheim, to strike at the juncture of Tallard's and Marsin's armies. The massive weight of his head-on cavalry charge broke the two apart. Each army turned in disorder toward its own center, with many soldiers pushed directly back into the Danube and drowned.

The charge was a model of the new style: close-formed lines, the riders knee to knee, advanced at a slow trot until they were almost upon the enemy, then broke into a furious gallop whose weight was enough to turn a flank or collapse a center, while the riders slashed right and left with their curved sabres.

Over the long, perilous hours the advantage shifted from side to side. A considerable number of charges failed. Three different times, Marsin pushed back attempted gains by Eugene, and French artillery missed its major mark by a hair's breadth when one of its cannon balls decapitated an officer holding a stirrup as Marlborough approached to take a fresh mount.

But by the end of the day the new tactics had proved themselves —along the entire front between Blenheim and Höchstädt a wild retreat was leaving a battleground strewn with French and Bavarian casualties. Some of them had died in place, either struck by the force of a cavalry charge, thrust through by the sabres of the riders, or penetrated by the dual-purpose guns with bayonets of the infantry that followed close behind.

The day ended with an episode that exceeded all others in the astonishment it caused when reported in the European capitals. In those days, the swift current of the free-flowing Danube ran close alongside Blenheim, below steep banks. In places, its width was as much as 300 feet. Early on, the commander Tallard had put in charge of his great aggregation of men had left them leaderless when, without explanation, he suddenly spurred his horse over the bank into the river. Both horse and rider drowned. Was he fleeing foreseen disgrace or seeking succor? No one ventured to say. Through the next hours, subordinate officers of the trapped French units attempted to break out. They failed because, using the river as its eastern segment, three of Marlborough's top generals had completed and were able to hold a ring enclosing the town.

The northern arc of the ring was already in place under Lord Cutts and as soon as Marlborough crossed the Danube, his brother Lt. Gen. Charles Churchill moved in to form a western arc. From Churchill's right over to the river bank, the Scottish Lt. Gen. Lord George Hamilton, Earl of Orkney, younger son of the third Duke of Hamilton, was in charge; he too had served with King William in Ireland and Flanders, and now with Marlborough. The circle was maintained and, at day's end when the charges and counter charges along the opposing lines in the fields to the west had subsided, it was Churchill who convinced this penned-in mass of prime French troops that their only option was surrender. Some 1,300 officers and 11,000 men became prisoners.

Before the surrender, Tallard had been attempting to reach Blenheim to extricate his men. As he forced his way toward them, an Allied soldier recognized him by the decoration on his uniform, the

Engraving of the Blenheim battleground at the end of the day.—*Trustees of the British Library*

Order of the St. Espirt, France's highest military honor. A few minutes later, France's highest military officer was a prisoner in English hands.

Since both Tallard and Marlborough had served their respective sovereigns as diplomats as well as generals, it was with the discourse of a diplomat that Marlborough shortly offered his ranking captive the use of his own coach while Tallard's was brought up from behind the French lines. The drama of the incident was so great that their exchange soon turned into direct discourse, the details of which passed from mouth to mouth in slightly variant forms, of which this one is found in a number of sources:

Marlborough: I am sorry that so great a catastrophy should have happened to a warrior for whom I entertain so high a respect.

Tallard: On my part, I congratulate you on having vanquished the best troops in the world.

Marlborough: Allow me to believe that mine are the best in the world, since they have conquered those whom you regard as such.

In France six interminable days dragged by (in the midst of the feasts and fireworks celebrating the birth of an heir to the duc de Bourgogne) before King Louis received an account of what had happened, beyond the bare fact of an enormous defeat. The Duc de Saint-Simon, whose *Historical Memoirs* cover much of the same period in France as John Evelyn's *Diary* does in England, wrote:

> The King received the bitter news on 21 August. . . . By that courier the King learned that a battle had taken place on the 13th, lasting from eight o'clock in the morning until dusk; that the Maréchal de Tallard's entire army was either dead or taken prisoner; that no one knew Tallard's own whereabouts, nor whether the Elector and Marsin had taken part in the action . . .
>
> Racked with anxiety, the King opened all the private letters, but he learned nothing from them, and remained for six days in the dreadful situation of knowing that all was lost in Bavaria, and yet unaware of what had happened. . . . Everything that anyone knew was tacked together, but even so no one could make head or tail of what had happened, and neither the King nor anyone else could imagine how an entire army, for such it was, placed in and around a village, could have been induced to sign a surrender. It was enough to make one's head reel.

Little by little the details began to filter through in the letters, and and on 20 August a French officer arrived, having been granted leave on parole by the Duke of Marlborough to give Louis Tallard's account of the disaster:

> We were not accustomed to defeat, and this one for sufficient reasons had been totally unexpected. It appeared, moreover, to have been the result of a series of monstrous errors, faulty plans, and panics. . . . You may readily imagine the dismay in France, where every noble family, not to mention the rest, had some member dead, wounded or missing . . . and the agony of the King, who so lately had the Emperor's fate within his grasp.[1]

The double impact of the capture of unprecedented numbers of prisoners at Blenheim and the capture of Louis XIV's commander-in-chief on his way to relieve the encircled town assured the name eventually fixed for Marlborough and Eugene's longed-for battle. For many years the French referred to the engagement as the battle of Höchstädt; but to the English, leaders and public alike, it was the battle of Blenheim, and their designation eventually dominated the history books.

The losses of this day were as unheard of as the tactics that caused them. Among Allied forces, the killed and wounded reached a total of some 12,000 men—nearly one in four of all they had. Of these, some 2,200 were British. But the French losses were some 40,000. The French officer corps had been shattered: of some 4,500 at the start, not more than 250 remained on active duty. More than 11,000 French and Bavarian prisoners had been taken; many more were captured during the long, pursued retreat, or slaughtered by infuriated peasants whose year's livelihood was gone. The Bavarian Elector followed the French back to his post as viceroy of the Netherlands, but later in the year, the Allies made a treaty with the Electress that brought Bavaria back under Imperial control.

While both sides had sustained unprecedented losses, the uneven ratio between them turned Blenheim into a lasting national French defeat rather than the loss of a summer's campaign. The results justified Marlborough's new concept of strategy.

In England, victory took away much of the sting of the casualty figures, though for the High Tories they continued to offer a convenient political issue. English engravers were quick to anticipate their public's enjoyment of the spectacle of Tallard and two other officers sitting in Marlborough's coach in comfortable misery, meditating on the answer to the question in all French minds: *Que dira le roi?* (What will the king say?) And German cartoonists in principalities on the Allied side gave equal pleasure with sketches of unhappy officers breaking the news to an allegorical figure of La Belle France.

An unnamed French aide-de-camp wrote his lament in a dispatch that was intercepted, taken to England, and published as a bilingual pamphlet. Of the surrender of standards at Blenheim, he mourned:

> They had much ado to get the consent of *Navarre,* who buried their Colours. All yielded. The Articles were sign'd: But *Siviere* and *Jourry* refused to set their Hands to it. They were all dis-arm'd, and their Colours taken from them: *Grief will not suffer me to carry this Recital any further.* [2]

For Marlborough and Eugene, August 13 N.S. had been a seventeen-hour working day. Saddles at two in the predawn dusk. Saddles all day, though the horses under them were not always the same. Saddles at the end of the afternoon, when the redcoats' final cavalry charge ended the engagement, with French contingents racing before it as they fled the field. And saddles still at six, when Marlborough gathered his chief officers on a little knoll for a preliminary assessment of the victory the new battle strategy had won.

Still on horseback, Marlborough borrowed from one of his companions a scrap of paper, a chit from the tavern that had served him a recent lunch. It was blank on one side. Laying it on a drum head held up to his saddle by a member of a regimental band, with a stubby pencil he scribbled the briefest of notes to Sarah:

Marlborough hands Parke the note to Queen Anne. Detail of engraving of Blenheim battleground.—*Trustees of the British Library*

August 13, 1704. I have not time to say more, but to beg you will give my Duty to the Queen, and let her know Her Army has had a Glorious Victory Mon[sr]. Tallard and two other Generals are in my coach and I am following the rest. the bearer, my Aid de Camp Coll. Parke will give Her and account of what has pass'd. I shal doe it in a day or two by another more att large

Marlborough.[3]

Calling up an aide, he handed him the note, with the instruction to take it to London, forthwith. The aide was Daniel Parke. His supreme moment of glory had arrived.

··

Chapter 12

Rider with the News

LIKE a red spark flying out of the Blenheim conflagration, Parke took the long road to Rotterdam. How many improvised relays enabled him to change exhausted horses is not known. What is known is that in a little over three days, he was there.

In his life of Marlborough, Winston Churchill calculates the distance over which the artillery dragged its guns from the starting point at Bedberg, northwest of Cologne, to Blenheim, southeast of Nürnberg, as some 420 miles. From Bedberg across Holland is at least 80 more. An unencumbered rider could and would take shortcuts where the big guns could not travel, and the latter part of the journey might be faster if made by water down the Rhine. However he did it, Parke covered the distance in record time.

He even made a few stops. At Frankfurt, Henry Davenant would be in touch with many of the secondary, as well as the primary, participants in the Alliance; and he was in constant communication with George Stepney, the experienced English envoy extraordinary then posted at Vienna. So Parke traveled some extra miles to give this diplomatic officer an eyewitness account of the final battle.

In the Netherlands, until Parke arrived, expectations from the present campaign had been minimal. On the day before the battle was fought at Blenheim a seasoned English observer and long-time diplomat, the earl of Stanhope, had written Stepney from The Hague:

Our Bavarian war seems not likely to be finished this year, and al hopes of reconsiliation are cutt off by the terrible destruction we have made in the Elector's Countrey, so that if her Majesty and the States do not resolve to let their Troopes winter there, they will lose the benefitt of all they have done hitherto.[1]

On the very next page of his letter book, this glumness was reversed to exultation by the same writer to the same correspondent on August 22 N.S., after Parke had passed:

There has not been in our age, or scarce to be found in Story, so compleat a victory as Prince Eugene and our Duke have gained over the Elector and Monsr. Tallard, which contrary to most others mends upon our hands and growes greater every day. . . . I fancy the great Monarch now in Augustus's condition after the defeat of Varus, tearing his flesh, stark mad and roaring out O Tallard, Tallard, rendez-moi mes Battalliones. [Give me back my ballalions!][2]

Such hyperbole was not to be expected of Davenant; from him, Stepney heard only the cautious estimate:

Yesterday Colonel Parke came here with the agreeable news of the victory we have gained over the enemies. This battle will in all appearance put an end to the war in the Empire, and give the means of assisting the Duke of Savoy who is very near his ruin. The Duke of Marlborough has beyond all dispute saved the Empire. Affairs were in no very good condition before this engagement.[3]

The Dutch lost no time in responding to Parke's news. In the mid-1650s, the United Provinces had had a silver medal struck to bestow as a parting gift to ambassadors leaving the country at the end of their terms of service. On its obverse, it bore the coat of arms of the Netherlands; on its reverse, the seven coats of arms of the constituent provinces. The motto around its rims read: RES PAR-

VAE CRESCUNT CONCORDIA, and DISCORDIA MAXIMAE DILABUNTUR. Two days after Parke's passage, the assembly of the States General voted to present him with one of these medals, in gold, affixed to a heavy gold chain of 1,500 guilders' value;* and, since Parke brought only the bare news of the victory, a second example was awarded to the Colonel Panton who arrived two days after Parke with the fuller description promised in Marlborough's note to Sarah. Given Parke's propensity for debt, it seems likely that the chain would eventually have been melted down; but that was not done immediately, for it appears in the portrait of its recipient painted by John Closterman a year or so later.

At Rotterdam, Parke was very lucky; he obtained an immediate passage across the North Sea, where the prevailing winds, blowing boisterously from southwest to northeast, not infrequently prevented departures for days on end. A four days' sail put him in London; on the eighth day after the Blenheim battle he was galloping to Marlborough House in St. James's to place her husband's note in Sarah's hand. Sarah read the tiny document, only to exclaim in dismay that the Queen was at Windsor. That meant another mount and another twenty-eight miles before completion of Parke's mission.

Some accounts say the Queen was playing with the little Prince of Wales on the terrace when the lone horseman galloped in, but the generally accepted view puts the scene later, after Her Majesty had gone to bed. In the royal family's private apartments, there is built into the tower overlooking the terrace, a tiny room that is now called the Blenheim Closet.** It was here that his sovereign received Parke in her dressing gown. As the bespattered messenger knelt before

---

*Gerhard van Loon published an engraving of this medal in his *Nederlandsche Historipenningen II* in 1726. The resolution passed by the States General on August 21, 1704, N.S. that granted Parke such a medal was published in 1936 by A. O. van Kerkwijk in the *Jahrboek voor Munt-en Penningkunde*, No. 23, as an appendix to his article on the ambassadors' medals, "De Verreeringpenningen door de Staten-General sedert 1628 toegekend." I am grateful to Dr. G. van der Meer for this information.

**The Blenheim Closet was then part of the row of rooms traditionally occupied by the distaff side of royalty, whether queen or consort; today it is part of the royal family's private library.

Dutch Ambassadors' Medal. The Dutch States General voted Daniel Parke a similar gold medal and chain as the bringer of the first news of the victory at Blenheim.—*Rijksmuseum Het Koninklijk Penningkabinet Leiden*

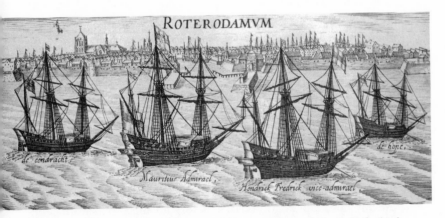

Maritime Rotterdam. The foreground shows a fleet of deep-draft, high-castled ships; the city's anchorages, in background, also harbored smaller "flyboats" used in navigating North Sea shoals. Parke would have taken one of these to London.—*Engraving from "Lof der Zeevaart," Collection of Dr. W. A. Engelbrecht, Maritiem Museum "Prins Hendrik," Rotterdam*

her, she read the scrap of paper handed him by the Duke on the battlefield. Slowly its full import sank into her consciousness, and anxieties of the years vanished. Her throne was secure. The Church to which she was deeply devoted was secure. And England was not only secure; it had become a new major independent power among the nations of Europe.

English messengers who brought great good news to their sovereign were traditionally awarded £500, but this time the overwhelmed Queen asked Parke what he would have. His bold answer was, a likeness of the Queen. It came, together with a purse of 1,000 guineas—an extravagance that drew a grumble from Marlborough —in a locket of gold encrusted with diamonds. For the rest of his life he wore it on a red ribbon, en cravate around his neck, over his uniform.

The tone of Marlborough's message resembles that of the little notes the Morleys and the Freemans were accustomed to exchange rather than a dispatch of a great commander to his sovereign. From Windsor, in the same vein, Anne wrote to Sarah:

> I have had the happiness of receiving my dear Mrs. Freeman's, by Colonel Parke, with the good news of this glorious victory, which, next to God Almighty, is wholly owing to dear Mr. Freeman, on whose safety I congratulate you with all my soul. May the same Providence that has hitherto preserved, still watch over, and send him home to you.[4]

Meanwhile, diplomatic observers lost no time transmitting dispatches to their capitals, while the English people engaged in a vast celebration. When Parke arrived, Signor Alvise Mocenigo of Venice, the dean of London's diplomatic corps accredited to the Court of St. James for over thirty-five years,* happened by sheer chance to be at Windsor. Apprised of Parke's message, after a night of reflection

---

*John Evelyn had been Mocenigo's host when he arrived to present his credentials in September 1668.

he was able to offer his government a few long-range comments in addition to a description of the nation's rejoicing. His dispatch was the first official account of the great news after it had been received by the Queen.

Mocenigo wrote:[*]

There arrived last night in great haste a messenger from the Duke of Marlborough's camp with news that the Allied armies had won a glorious victory over the enemy. The news does not give details of the battle; it contains greetings from the Duke to the Duchess . . . and mentions that he is still on horseback and about to attempt to overtake the fleeing army. . . . She is to inform the Queen of the victory, and tell her that the Count de Tallard and two other generals are prisoners in his carriage. . . . Another aide will give a more precise accounting in a day or two.

Mocenigo mistakenly expected that after meeting with Tallard, the Elector of Bavaria would reinforce an offensive; but he farsightedly stressed that while "London let its extreme happiness be known, attention was paid to the fact that because what had happened was of great consequence to all Europe, it would be proclaimed that the present governmental system was safe."[5]

Although the Dutch envoy to London, L'Hermitage, bore a French surname, the finer points of the language of diplomacy suggested by his parentage never ceased to cause him difficulties. Bravely, however, he used the correct medium of reporting to inform his government that Parke had arrived between three and four in the afternoon and, as he passed through London on his way to Windsor, had shared the news of the great victory. Only moments later, he said, the Tower bells were set a-ringing, and bonfires and illumina-

---

[*] I am grateful to Dr. George B. Daniel, Professor of Romance Languages in the University of North Carolina at Chapel Hill, for a translation of the Venetian envoy's letter of August 11/12, 1704.

tions lit up the sky as soon as darkness fell. The news supplanted all others, and no one concerned himself with anything else.[6]

London's biweekly news sheet, *The Observator*, for Saturday August 12–Wednesday August 16 O.S. used three of its four columns for a mock interview that began:

> *Observator:*   Oh Brave Countryman, thou lookest Merrily, like a Man again; thou has been in the Dumps a long time . . .
> *Country-man:*   I look like a Man again? Aye, like a Prince of a Man! . . . I am grown as Fat as a Pig, the Duke of *Marlborough* has fed me with Fighting Stories till my Jowls are grown as red as a *Turky* Cocks. I am grown so Brisk that I can leap over a House.[7]

Printed copies of Marlborough's note to Sarah were struck off; they sold like hotcakes at London booksellers' and flew like carrier pigeons deep into the countryside. As far away as Melbourne in Derbyshire, Thomas Coke, M.P. received two letters with similar contents dated August 10, giving the bare bones of the news:

> As we were sitting down to dinner at my masters came a copy of my Lord Marlborough's letter to the Dutchesse, sent by his Ayd-de-camp Colonel Parker [sic]. He says only that he had entirely defeated French and Bavarians, and that Tallard and two other generals were then prisoners in his coach. He refers himself for particulars to Parker; but he cannot give many, as to place of action and number of those engaged. He came away just as the victory was declared, and my lord M. was giving orders for the pursuit. The letter was writ on horseback with a black leaden pencil. The victory was gained on the 2nd of August, our style. Parker has rode it in eight days.[8]

In John Evelyn's diary for August 10, he was careful to claim kin with his cousin:

> This weeke brought over hapy newes of the French & Bavarian Armys defeate by the Confederats. . . . This was immediatly

brought to the Queene, during the yet pursuite of the Enemys, written & sent by my Co: Parcke (an officer & Ayde de Camp) by the D: of Marlboro in such extreme hast, as he could not particularly describe the rest of the Circumstances & Event, which we hourely expect: ... there is no thing but triumphs & demonstrations of Joy in the Citty & every where.[9]

A line in Marlborough's letter written on September 3 N.S. to Robert Harley, Speaker of the House of Commons, "I was glad to see that Parke had brought you the good news of our victory," shows that the messenger had been debriefed at top levels. The Duke's private note to Godolphin, reviewing the yield gained during his pursuit of the French after the battle itself was over,* wryly remarks that even "No. 17" will allow it to have been a victory. No. 17 was their code for the earl of Nottingham, who, together with the Queen's uncle Lord Rochester, was among the High Tories most bitterly opposed to the war.[10]

For that mid-August interval, the glory that Parke had hoped for was his in full measure. High and low, the Parke name was on every tongue; his father would have been delighted. Since he was the only person in London who had been present on the field, he was flatteringly sought after. The interval was brief: on the evening of August 13 the Lord Tunbridge arrived with the fuller account that the Duke had promised. By August 22 O.S., Parke, laden with dispatches, was on his way to rejoin his commander on the continent. By September 6 N.S. he had arrived at headquarters.[11] But he had made a sensation in the capital.

After the good news had been relished by all classes came the official thanksgiving. The new St. Paul's had been opened by a service of celebration for the Peace of Ryswick in 1697; with Marlborough's

---

*On September 27, O.S. Evelyn's diary also extols the "Still greater Confirmations of the Confederats Victory, the D. of Bavaria quite beaten out of his Country, who now sent their deputys to the Emp, to crave his protection & rescue their Country from utter Spoile. ... The Prisoners & spoile divided into 3 parts, to the Emp, English & Dutch: tis estimated the Fr: lost 40000 men kild & Taken, such a defeate as never was given in Europ these 1000 years."

succession of victories, this church became the official site for the expression of England's public gratitude for secular events. During Queen Anne's reign, there were eight such occasions, the first in 1704 and the last in 1713, on the signing of the Treaty of Utrecht. Queen Anne's presence graced all but the last, when her health forced her to "give thanks to God for peace in her own closet." To this day, on such occasions, the position of the sovereign as head of the Church of England is acknowledged in the arrangements for the ceremony.

The nineteenth-century historian, John Hill Burton, described the plan of Queen Anne's chamberlain for the celebration of 1704. Because the Privy Council had voted that the cathedral was to be considered the Chapel Royal for the day, the chamberlain proclaimed that the Queen's throne should duplicate the one on which she sat in the House of Lords. It should be about three feet higher than the floor of the choir, covered with a Persian carpet, with an armchair for a throne, a foot stool in front of it, a desk for the Queen's book, covered with crimson velvet embroidered and fringed with gold, beside it, and a canopy, securely fixed, was to be mounted overhead.[12]

On September 7 all London lined the streets along the route from St. James's Palace to Ludgate Hill. Evelyn's diary gives the details: the Queen paraded in a coach-and-eight, unaccompanied except for the Duchess of Marlborough in a very plain garment; the Queen full of jewels. Crown officers, nobility, bishops followed in coaches-and-six. Music and trumpets were everywhere. Awaiting the procession at Temple Bar, the City companies were ranged under their banners alongside rails hung with cloth consonant in color with the banners. The Lord Mayor, sheriffs, and aldermen were in their scarlet robes, mounted on caparisoned horses. And, to complete the occasion, the weather was the finest of the year.[13]

Marlborough himself had no part in the earlier English celebrations, though at this time he received a message from Vienna that Leopold I's gratitude for Blenheim was to be expressed in his elevation of Marlborough to be a prince of the Holy Roman Empire with

Sarah Jennings, first Duchess of Marlborough (1660–1744). Engraving by John Faber I (1650–1721), after a painting by Kneller.
—*Trustees of the British Museum*

Queen Anne (1665–1714), Queen Regnant (1702–1714). This portrait, which hangs in the Assembly Room of the Williamsburg capitol today, continues the old tradition of keeping a likeness of her there, that began with the completion of the building. The first portrait may have been displayed as a result of Parke's request to the Perrys early in the reign to obtain such a portrait from the Lords of Trade and Plantations. The currently displayed canvas is attributed to the School of Sir Godfrey Kneller.
—*Colonial Williamsburg Foundation*

a tiny principality of his own—an honor that, however received in England, would bring him prestige throughout central Europe.

Before coming home, the general returned to the Rhine and besieged the fortress of Landau above Phillipsburg; his plan for 1705 was to strike directly at France along the Moselle. Then, to keep Alliance participants content, his coach bumped him over the frozen ruts of northern Europe for consultations with confederated heads of state. So it was December before he accepted the congratulations of Parliament, attended an even more colorful ceremony than that of September at St. Paul's, and received from Queen and country the gift of the estate and the great Vanbrugh-designed palace at Woodstock that today bears the name of his decisive battle.

By this time England's semiannual fleet had delivered the good news to the American colonies. In Virginia, Francis Nicholson, now long enough restored to the Virginia governorship to be generous to the man with whom he had threatened to duel a decade earlier, issued a proclamation calling for a day of "publick and solemn thanksgiving"—though not so solemn as to preclude a display of the militia and the firing of three volleys of rejoicing after the sermon:

> Whereas, it had pleased almighty God to grant to her Maj^te armes in Conjunction with her allys . . . a Signall & glorious victory . . . (the first account whereof being brought to her most Sacred Majesty by Coll. Parke, a Gent & native of this Country . . .) and the R^t Honble the Lords Com^is for trade and plantancons, having been pleased to send unto me her Maj^te Royal proclamacon for a day of thanksgiveing . . . with direccons to me to appoint a proper & speedy day of thanksgiveing, to be kept . . . ^within this her Maj^tes Colony and Dominion of Virg^a Therefore I, ffr. Nicholson, . . . do recommend to the Ministers of the respective parishes, that as soon as the proclamacon shall reach them, they take notice of the same.[14]

Parke's old neighbors were impressed; thereafter, various Virginians gave the name of Blenheim to new plantations, and the town of Marlborough was founded as a port on the Potomac.

In London Parke sat for several of the beau monde's favorite painters. A private purchase has removed Sir Godfrey Kneller's likeness of him from public view, but George Vertue's engraving of it was used on the front page of a pamphlet in 1717. A photograph of another privately owned painting, by Michael Dahl, is in the possession of the National Portrait Gallery in London. All of these display the locket containing Parke's miniature of the Queen. So do the two three-quarter-length portraits that were painted by John Closterman, which descended to Parke's daughters. Both are in existence in Virginia now, one of them in the collections of the Virginia Historical Society. The Closterman portraits also show, draped over a breastplate of black armor on a table to the right of the standing figure, a heavy gold chain with three medals attached. The chain and the foremost medal were the gift of the Netherlands government to the aide-de-camp who brought the good news, "de eerste tydinge van de victorie," to Holland. The other medals were given by other continental allies.

As he posed for the artists depicting him, Parke relished in anticipation the reward he thought the public response to his ride had made reliably certain.

Chapter 13

The Lesser Reward

AND then, suddenly, fact failed to match fantasy. In the weeks of exhilaration after the ride, fantasy had whispered to the rider that surely, when the Crown distributed the bounties of the Blenheim victory, fulfillment of his life's ambition would be realized. What other officer's uniform could display a miniature of his Queen?

Several years later, Parke was improbably asserting that on the very battlefield Marlborough had promised him the governorship of Virginia. He did not receive it. He had indeed been one of the Great Duke's aides-de-camp, and it did indeed fall to his lot to carry the news of his commander's greatest victory to the Queen. But the officers and men who did the fighting were the winners of the victory; and among the officers one general had special and overriding claims to the Virginia post.

On the Blenheim battlefield, it was the Earl of Orkney who had held the most difficult segment of the ring that kept the French battalions squeezed into the river town. And while this was in itself enough, there was a further basis for the appointment of Orkney as chief governor and captain general of Virginia; he was a Scot.* The award of this honor justly celebrated the past, but it had the additional advantage of supporting important English policy for the im-

---

*The man who, under Orkney, became Virginia's next lieutenant governor was also a Scot: Alexander Spotswood had been the army's deputy quartermaster general at Blenheim.

Lord George Hamilton, Earl of Orkney (1666–1737) and chief governor and captain general of Virginia, 1714–1737. Hamilton was given the post that Parke wanted. Engraved in 1742 by Jacobus Haubraken after portrait by Martin Maingaud.—*Virginia Historical Society*

mediate future. For several years, negotiations had been under way between England and Scotland looking toward a union of the two nations; an official agreement would complete the union of the two crowns effected in 1603 when James VI of Scotland, on the death of Queen Elizabeth, became James I, sovereign of the United Kingdom.

Agreement on the fusion of the two nations required delicate treatment of very sensitive issues; in the course of the talks, the chances of a successful outcome had swayed back and forth like a pendulum. Politically, agreement had been reached that the Scots, while retaining their own church and legal structures, would legislate in a common Parliament, in which Scotland would be represented by sixteen Scottish peers and forty-five elected members of the House of Commons. But the Scots were no less concerned about their economic prospects; they exerted enough pressure for the English Parliament, in the very year of Blenheim, to pass a Security Act affirming that Scottish merchants would trade as equals in the newly formed nation and the empire.

In such touch-and-go circumstances, the English bestowal of a signal honor on a member of a ranking Scottish family offered considerable leverage; but award of a post recognizably related to Scotland's position in the soon-to-be-united economy would carry a special value. In this respect the governorship of Virginia had measurable luster, for among the chief possibilities for mercantile profit that the Scots especially desired was profit from the legal importation and resale of American tobacco, sure to be considerably larger than their present yield from smuggling operations. Virginia and Maryland were the principal producers of this commodity under the English flag and the prospect of having one of their own peers as governor of such a source was eagerly relished by the canny Glasgow merchants poised to become the tobacco dons of the rising century.

The Scotsman Commissary Blair, was in London at the time, and exhibited his usual power to assess realities in a letter to Philip Ludwell:

There is little new; only that it is in everybody's mouth that the government of Virg^a was to be given to my Lord Orkney. My Lord has been entertained with renewed promises, but the thing is not yet declared; some say the delay has been occasioned by some heats in Parliament, relating to Scotland, about the succession which are not yet quite over, but are likely to end in an offer of a Union to that kingdom: others think they are waiting to have Govr Nicholson's answers to all the papers and affidavits which were sent him from hence. . . . As for my own opinion, if I were to venture a wager, it should be y^t my Lord Orkney will be declared Governor.[1]

In the event, Orkney's appointment remained for long an informal understanding: a decade was to pass before the actual papers were officially signed and sealed.

Though he retained the gubernatorial title until his death in 1737, Orkney himself never visited his colony. Even his first deputy, Alexander Spotswood, did not reach Williamsburg until 1710. Too much was going on: Orkney served with his accustomed brilliance under Marlborough again and again throughout the long war—he was at Ramillies in 1706, Oudenarde in 1708, and Malplaquet in 1709. The Peace of Utrecht was not signed until 1713, and Orkney's gubernatorial commission is dated December 17, 1714.

During the first part of the interim, Francis Nicholson governed Virginia. He had been restored to his previous place as soon as Blair had succeeded in maneuvering Andros out of it. He held office until 1705, when he too was recalled at the instance of the commissary. Blair's seniority as president of the Council—he died at eighty-eight —gave him an unequaled period of influence in Virginia affairs. Nonetheless, his reversal of position on Nicholson occasioned a certain amount of merriment in the form of "A Ballad Addressed to the Revd Members of the Convocation Held at Mann's Ordinary, at Williamsburgh & Virginia":

> Bless us what dismal times are these,
> What stars are in conjunction,

When Priests turn Sycophants to please,
And Hair brained Passion to appease,
    Dare Prostitute their Function.

Sure all the Furies must combine,
    To Sway the Convocation,
When 17 Clergymen should join,
Without one word of Proof to Sign,
    So false an accusation.

Or rather some for interest,
    And hopes of next preferment,
By false pretences finely dress'd,
Slyly imposed upon the rest,
    To sign on their averment . . .

The Tavern was the place they chose,
    To hold their consultation,
Where each one drank a lusty dose,
His Stupid Coxcombe to dispose,
    To form the accusation.

Good Store of Bristol Beer & Stout
    By dozens was expended,
The Glass went merrily about,
Some Sung & others swore & fought,
    And so the farce was ended.

Blest state to which the orders sunk,
    A happy reformation,
Now without fear they may be drunk,
And fight & swear & keep a Punk,
    And laugh at deprivation.[2]

Early rumors, however, had caused Nicholson much uneasiness; they spread the possibility that his old enemy from the mid-1690's might take over his office. On August 24, 1704, the rarely mistaken collector of news of public affairs, Narcissus Luttrell, was in error. He entered in his calendar the statement that "Her majestie has been

Section of map of the Caribbean islands, showing Daniel Parke's province, the Leeward Islands: St. Kitts, Barbuda, Nevis, Antigua, and Montserrat. From Bryan Edwards, *The History, Civil and Commercial, of the British Colonies in the West Indies (1801).—Folger Shakespeare Library*

pleased to promise the government of Virginia to collonel Parke, in the room of collonel Nicholson who will be removed." He corrected this error the following March 8: "Collonel Parks, who brought the first news of the victory at Hockstet, is made governor of the Leeward Islands, in the room of Collonel Matthews, deceas'd."[3]

Meanwhile, Nicholson had written the Board of Trade that it was first "industriously reported through the Country that there will be a new Governor a-coming, and . . . that Col. Parke was to be the Governor. . . . Then afterwards they said that when he asked for it, he was told he had come some hours too late . . . that the Earl of Orkney, a Scotch nobleman, was made Governor."[4]

The reward Parke actually received did make him a royal governor. But instead of Virginia, his charge was to be one part of the

English holdings in the little chain of West Indian islands that forms the eastern boundary of the Caribbean Sea. The name of the place itself was a mockery, for these islands are part of the Lesser Antilles, and are small: the black heights that protrude above the ocean waters in an oval began as the steep peaks of ancient volcanos. Each island is ringed with a wreath of decayed lava, fertile ground for abundant harvests of tropical specialties, but each island lives under annual threat of drought or hurricane. All of the group that constituted Parke's province were tiny: among the four largest, Antigua has an area of just over 100 square miles.

The Lesser Antilles governments did not have a chief governor and captain general who could reside in London without ever setting foot in his colony. The governor of Parke's province was expected to fulfill a role similar to that of a lieutenant governor of Virginia: to go to the capital and take active charge. As a capital, St. John's, Antigua, did not compare favorably with Williamsburg, Virginia.

An effusive letter Parke wrote to Marlborough on July 26, 1705, has the aspect of an anchor cast to windward. He clearly sounds as though he still hoped for an appointment more to his liking:

> Had I thought I should have staid in England this Summer for want of a Ship I wou'd have done myselfe the Honour to have waited on your Grace this campaigne, and there have Express'd Gratitude for all the goodness you have been pleased to show me; I am not without hopes yett of getting a Ship to transport me to that post wch I ow singly to your Grace's countinence and favour, but before I quit England I must beg leave once more to assure your Grace of my Eternal Gratitude, and to wish that Every moment of your Life may produce to you fresh Honours and New Glory, this being all the Contribution he is Able to make who Esteems it his Chief Happiness to be
>
> My Lord
> Your Graces most Humble
> and most Obliged Servant . . .[5]

Many holders of Caribbean governorships met the requirements currently favored in Whitehall for administrators of the growing empire. And, if governors generally accepted such appointments with a view to accumulating personal fortunes as they upheld their sovereign's prerogative, the colonists showed a certain understanding, since that was a major purpose of their own. But the settlers tended to assess new governors with an eye to the extent to which they adapted their perquisites to private gain, and to complain to Whitehall with vigor when, in their judgment, the office was being too exclusively employed for the governor's private enhancement.

Like many another disappointed officeholder, Daniel Parke dawdled in London, repeatedly postponing his departure. His appointment had been announced in March 1705; Queen Anne had signed his instructions in June; and the seal to be affixed to the province's official business was delivered to him in the first part of August. He did not take ship, however, until late spring, 1706.

During the last months of 1705, from his house in Hampshire, he again tried his luck at parliamentary politics, this time standing for Whitchurch. Had he been successful, he might have withdrawn his name from the Caribbean appointment and remained in London to perform his parliamentary duties while seeking domestic preferment or a different overseas post. But again there was alleged wrongdoing at Whitchurch, and the circumstances were once more brought to the attention of the House of Commons. Although there were no allegations of wrongdoing against Parke, manipulation of the election brought him another defeat. The parliamentary *Journals* record receipt of a petition from nine freeholders and burgesses of the borough declaring that in the recent contest between Daniel Parke, John Shrimpton, and Richard Wollaston, Esquires, the petitioners "had a Right to vote at such Election, and offered their Votes for Mr. *Parke;* but *James Butler,* the Mayor, refused their Votes, and yet admitted several to vote for Mr. Wollaston, that had no right to vote, and hath arbitrarily returned Mr. Wollaston though he was not duly elected."[6]

Since Parke, they said, had not petitioned for relief, these free-holders "are apprehensive, that, by an Acquiescency under such illegal Proceedings, they may be deprived of their Rights of voting at future Elections," and ask consideration of their case by the House. According to Luttrell, Parke did enter a petition on his own behalf against Mr. Wollaston's election, in reply to which the House ordered that he be heard at the bar. A hearing was ordered for December 4, but there is no record of further consideration, and the matter lapsed.[7]

At the same time that things were going badly for Parke in the mother country, word came that his affairs were in equally poor shape at Queen's Creek plantation in Virginia. A startling communication from Jane Parke, dated July 12, 1705, reached London with the autumn ships. It announced her resignation.

A four-month bout of illness, she said, had left her physically unable to carry on the burden of plantation management that she had borne for most of what passed for their married life. Bitterly, she stated that "It is impossible for me to be further serviceable to you." She reminded Parke that over the years he had complained of the size of the yield of the plantation, making her "wonder how you think we live, especially you that have lived so like a man of quality all your life, and know so well how a gentlewoman should live."[8]

Most of her long plaint concerns the future of the children, especially their daughters. Referring to Julius Caesar as "your godson," she reported that he had finished his year at the college, though if Parke were to look at him he "would not believe he ever have had one hour's study bestowed upon him. I must confess I am ashamed to think I have had eight years' care of him to so little purpose. I am unwilling to speak much of his temper, lest you should think it prejudice in me."

She was indignant that Parke had taken no steps with regard to marriages for the daughters; the girls, she says, do not even know whether their father plans their future on this side of the Atlantic or the other. In a society in which most girls married at sixteen, their eldest is "wanting but two months of entering her twentieth year, the younger one well gone on her eighteenth." She has had no reply from him to her query as to his attitude toward an offer made to the elder. His instructions forbidding them to receive callers at their home is causing them to put off the best suitors in the country; and the fact that prospective swains have asked the girls to meet them elsewhere has caused her to "reflect on the results of too much restraint as well as those of too much liberty."

She has had the girls take dancing lessons and is on the point of starting them in French. They have no new clothes except a suit apiece, which she has made herself: "This is what I could not avoid doing for them to have them look tolerable like other people."

Jane closes with the "hope, when this comes to hand, that you will consider it, and let me know your resolution." As she has previously told him, she would like to be relieved of further responsibilities and cares, have a pittance to live on, and retire to a quiet place.

According to Mary Custis Lee, who inherited the Parke correspondence, Jane had previously written similar letters to Parke, as well as to Micajah Perry urging him to influence Parke to return to Virginia. This one carried an air of finality that may have been more insistent than the others. Nonetheless, no response is to be found among surviving correspondence. From his departure in 1697 until his death thirteen years later, Parke never returned to Virginia.

∴

Chapter 14

Double Wedding

JANE Parke need not have worried about the girls. When her husband finally took passage for the Caribbean colony he was to govern, it was on a date that placed him at sea, rather than at his Virginia plantation, when his daughters were married in a doubly distinguished double wedding on May 4, 1706. In the eyes of Tidewater society, both of the girls married very well. Although their father had made none of the usual efforts on their behalf, his exploit in rushing the good news of Blenheim from the Danube up the Neckar, down the Rhine, across the North Sea, and from London to Windsor had lost no glamor in the tale's repetition. A few of the men in public life during the previous decade—perhaps Commissary Blair?—might cherish old scores against this rider, but for most, colonial squabbles were lost in the sweep of imperial history.

In London, Virginians of prominence had been present in 1704 to witness the royal processions and services of thanksgiving in all their color; and they joined in the adulation of Parke in those first days when he alone could give an eyewitness account of the great battle. Among them was the thirty-year-old William Byrd II, whose long presence as an ornament of London society was abruptly interrupted in 1705 by news of his father's death the previous December; it necessitated his return to the colony to become executor of the family fortune. Through him and others, the story of Parke's ride spread by word of mouth across Tidewater. It was foreseeable that he would look up Parke's family.

In Jane's concern that her daughters were passing—indeed had almost passed—the age of prime eligibility, she had not anticipated such publicity. Before long, Parke was receiving letters from or on behalf of two highly eligible young men who sought permission to "address" the young ladies.

Such letters were expected, and served to determine the attitude of the father toward a given match. (Without a favorable response, elopement became the remaining alternative, and it was both socially undesirable and potentially costly, since it left the question of a dowry unsettled.) In seeking permission to declare himself to the object of his affections (who was usually fully aware of the young gentleman's feelings), the prospective bridegroom was expected to give his potential father-in-law an account of his current financial position and his future prospects. If paternal approval were granted, the father was in turn expected to indicate what he proposed in the way of endowment of the bride.

William Byrd II found Parke's younger daughter, Lucy, entrancing. Since his recent inheritance had proclaimed him one of the wealthiest men in Virginia, it was unnecessary—indeed it would have been ostentatious—to make specific reference to his worldly prospects. He merely said, "I don't question but my fortune may be sufficient to make her happy, especially after it has been assisted by your bounty." But otherwise he followed convention even to the extent of a coy affectation of concealment of the name of the person approached—he called Parke "Signor Fanfaroni":

> Since my arrival in this country I have had the honour to be acquainted with your daughters, and was infinitely surpriz'd to find young ladys with their accomplishments in Virginia. This surprize was soon improv'd into a passion for the youngest for whom I have all the respect and tenderness in the world.

However I think it my duty to interest your approbation before
I proceed to give her the last testimony of my affection.

The waiting period required for mail to cross the Atlantic, be answered, and return to Virginia seemed in these circumstances more
unbearable than usual; Byrd wrote Lucy:

> O the torture of six months' expectation! If it must be so long,
> and necessity will till then interpose betwixt you and my in-
> clinations, I must submit, though it be as unwillingly as pride
> submits to superior virtue, or envy to superior succes. Pray
> think of me and believe that Veramour is entirely and eternally
> yours.

In anticipation of a reply about which neither could have had any
real doubts, Byrd continued his outpourings to his "Fidelia," mix-
ing his London sophistication with the more usual declarations of a
love-smitten swain:

> No courtier can gape for preferment with more impatience than
> I do to hear from my charming Fidelia.
> May angels guard my dearest Fidelia and deliver her safe to
> my arms at our next meeting: and sure they wont refuse their
> protection to a creature so pure and charming, that it would
> be easy for them to mistake her for one of themselves. If you
> could but believe how entirely you possess the impire of my
> heart, you would easily credit me, when I tell you, that I can
> neither think nor so much as dream of any other subject than
> the enchanting Fidelia.[1]

Fanny's suitor was John Custis, the fourth of that name in Virginia. His age and Byrd's were within four years of each other;
perhaps because the familiar portrait of him was not painted until
1725, when he was forty-seven, the impression he makes is rather
that of a capable squire than a gallant young blade. His personality
resembled that of the first Daniel Parke of Virginia, with its acu-

men for making purchases and its careful attention to bookkeeping. His father had prudently set aside money for his education; he was sent to England to complete it, and while in residence there received seven years of business training in the firm of Perry & Lane.

Yet when the time came to write Parke a letter proposing marriage to Parke's elder daughter, even though John Custis IV was twenty-seven years old, because finances were involved it was John Custis III who wrote the request and received Parke's reply:

London, August 25, 1705

Sir: I received yours relating to your son's desire of marrying my daughter, and your consent if I thought well of it. You may easily inform yourself that my daughter, Frances, will be heiress to all the land my father left, which is not a little, or the worst. My personal estate is not very small in that country, and I have but two daughters, and there is no likelihood of my having any more, as matters are, I being obliged to be on one side of the ocean, and my wife on the other. I do not know your young gentleman, nor have you or he thought fit to send me an account of his real and personal effects; however, if my daughter likes him, I will give her upon her marriage with him, half as much as he can make appear he is worth.

I have no one else to give my estate to but my daughters. This is what I think convenient to write at present. My service to you and all friends in Virginia.

From your humble servant,

To Colonel Custis. Daniel Parke.[2]

So all was agreed, and with Jane's Ludwell kinsmen serving as hosts at Greenspring, her daughters were married.

The news, in particular of Byrd's espousal, caused a stir in London, whose belles had lost an assiduous squire. Helena Le Grand, daughter of Sir Robert Southwell, Byrd's counselor from his early youth, wrote her cousin, the future earl of Egmont and Byrd's life-

William Byrd II of Westover (1674–1744), by unknown artist.
—*Virginia Historical Society*

John Custis IV of Arlington (1678–1749), by unknown
American artist.—*Washington/Custis/Lee Collection, Washington and Lee University*

long friend, "I writ you in my last I think of Mr. Byrd's marriage in Virginia. They say his wife is as handsome as the Dutchess of Bolton, so he may rest satisf'd for his share."[3]

In 1702 a warning about marriage had been part of the letter in which Parke announced to Fanny his decision to turn to a military career: "I know that it is the desire of all young people to be married, and though few are so happy after marriage as before, yet every one is willing to make the experiment at their own expense."[4]

His doubts about the likelihood of postmarital bliss were borne out in the subsequent history of both couples. Financial difficulties, most of them due to Parke's own behavior, had made their appearance within six months of the wedding. Parke reneged on his commitment to John Custis, Sr., in respect to Frances's dowry, and left unpaid the £1,000 he had promised for Lucy. On December 5, 1706, the long-suffering Micajah Perry informed the Custis bridegroom that he had tried his best to get a response, but so far still awaited Parke's reply:

> I rejoyce that Coll. Parke hath gott over his illnesse in the west Indias: god give him health and send his ships saffe to us from him: Every houer we Expect them and if soe I yet hope to se he will act the part of a ffather: to both the Young Ladeys I have his repeated ingagmts he will doe soe: and tho I am very unhappy in all I advise: yet will run the Hazzard.[5]

A year later, Philip Ludwell II, then living in England, had a further talk with Mr. Perry, and wrote a long letter to his son, Philip III in Virginia; in it he discussed the girls' mother's future as well as their own:

> I know Mr. Perry and Park both watch whether I will take her into my care. Mr. Perry, (like a good charitable man) has as good as told me not only that, but to give portions to the girles to. If they find I am inclined that way, I must question whether they would allow her a farthing.[6]

Parke was apparently repudiating his elder daughter's marriage on the grounds that Frances had married beneath her. Ludwell's acid comment was, "I take Custis to be of as good extraction as Byrd or Park himself."[7]

Ludwell said he would have another talk with Perry and forecast his future provision for his sister by asking his son-in-law to furnish him with a complete account of the Parke estate's current yield. "After that, if Park or Mr. Perry will not allow her what is reasonable it may be I may take a course for it may not be very advantageous to his Excellency but I would not have her . . . really in want."[8]

As soon as the wedding festivities were over, Jane resigned her responsibilities. The Custises took over the house at Queen's Creek, and thereafter Parke allowed Custis a fifth of the net yield for managing the cultivation of his plantations. Jane, as Philip, Sr., had foreseen, moved to Greenspring to pass the short remainder of her life there. When she died in September 1708 Philip Ludwell III sent word to London: "She was taken with a cold shivering which was succeeded by a feavour which never left her til it ended with her live. . . . We had the best advise we could gett, but when God calls the best Phisitians skill will not availe."[9]

On November 3, 1709, Byrd's diary notes, "I waited on the ladies to Queen's Creek where my mother Parke's things were divided between my wife and her sister."[10] The inventory of the Queen's Creek plantation shows the near-poverty in which Parke's family had lived; item after item is qualified as "old," "worn," "broken," "dirty, stained, and very much patched."[11]

In the way of marital quarrels, Byrd's tiffs with Lucy were transient compared to the genuine hatred that developed between Fanny and John Custis. The coded diary that Byrd began to keep at Westover in 1709 contains rather frequent entries regarding friction between him and Lucy; but the causes were usually petty and the resolutions rapid.

He found Lucy extravagant: on June 14, 1709 he notes "In the evening the boat returned and brought some letters for me from England, with an invoice of things sent [for?] by my wife which are enough to make a man mad. It put me out of humor very much. I neglected to say my prayers, for which God forgive me." [12]

Their most serious disagreements occurred when Lucy was unkind and sometimes cruel to the slaves who attended her. But the general temper of their relationship is illustrated by a squabble that occurred as the couple was preparing to go to the capital to enjoy the Governor's Ball and other festivities that surrounded a Council meeting:

> My wife and I quarreled about her pulling her brows. She threatened she would not go to Williamsburg if she might not pull them; I refused, however, and got the better of her, and maintained my authority. . . . My cold grew exceedingly bad so that I thought I should be sick. . . . I rose about 9 o'clock but was so bad I thought I should not have been in condition to go to Williamsburg, and my wife was so kind to [say] she would stay with me, but rather than keep her from going I resolved to go if possible. I was shaved with a very dull razor, and ate some boiled milk for breakfast but neglected to say my prayers. About 10 o'clock I went to Williamsburg without the ladies.

Another such "terrible quarrel" occurred when Lucy was again abusing a slave. Byrd stoically recorded that she "gave me abundance of bad words and endeavored to strangle herself, but I believe in jest only. However, after acting a mad woman a long time she was passive again. . . . At night we drank some cider by way of reconciliation." [13]

In terms of the wifely duties that were socially regarded as of paramount importance, Lucy accomplished only half, but it was a generous half indeed. The best of wives were expected to produce a male heir and at least one beautiful daughter. Lucy's second child was a boy named Parke Byrd, but he died in early infancy. Their daughter Evelyn, however, became a toast of two continents.

From babyhood, Evelyn's father found her exquisite. In the first year of a diary containing few references to the children, he celebrated on July 16, "This day my daughter Evelyn is two years old. Pray God send his blessing on her." And that October, in a letter to John Custis, he announced that "Miss Evelyn has grown a great romp, and enjoys very robust health." By the time she became a young lady, Byrd, once more in England, sent for her and, after worrying at length about the safety of her passage, wrote pridefully, "My daughter Evelyn has arrived safe, thank God, and I hope I shall manager her in such a manner that she may be no discredit to her country."[14]

But when the time came for marriage proposals, her father did not find her manageable. He refused to countenance the approach of the titled Englishman on whom her heart was set. Due to the use of fanciful names in correspondence, this "Mr. Effendi" has never been identified and she refused all others. At thirty she died at Westover, unwed.

By contrast to the minor frictions between Byrd and Lucy, the tensions that developed between Frances and John Custis over the years were serious and lasting. An enduring, if perhaps apocryphal, Virginia legend summarizes their relations in a tale of an outing while they were living on the Custis family plantation on Virginia's Eastern Shore. The design of the house afforded them separate quarters; even when both were present they communicated in messages carried back and forth by slaves. In the dining room, they consumed their meals in bristling silence. Then one afternoon Custis surprisingly proposed that they go for a drive together. As told by one of many collectors of Virginia legends, after helping her to her seat he headed the horses first toward Chesapeake Bay—and then into it.

When the water was above the floor boards, Frances asked, "Where are you going, Colonel Custis?" "To hell, madam," he replied. "Drive on," she answered, "any place is better than Arlington." Custis turned the carriage around and drove her home. Finally in June 1714, they drew up an agreement whereby Frances agreed

Evelyn Byrd (1707–1737), daughter of Lucy Parke Byrd, by unknown artist.
—*Colonial Williamsburg Foundation*

Frances Parke Custis (1686–1715), by unknown artist.—*Washington/Parke/Lee Collection, Washington and Lee University*

to return her husband's money, plate, and other things "that she hath taken from him," and she promised never to do it again. She also agreed that she would not call John "any vile names or give him any ill language." Custis promised not to abuse his wife and to give her half of the profits from the estate to manage the household. Each agreed to live "lovingly together and to behave themselves as a good husband and good wife ought to doe."[15]

While this tale is doubtless only symbolically accurate, a final account of their relationship is set in stone. When John Custis died, his will commanded his son, on pain of disinheritance, to cause the following inscription to be carved on his monument. It may be seen in the graveyard today:

UNDER THIS MARBLE TOMB LIES THE BODY

OF THE HON. JOHN CUSTIS, ESQ.,

OF THE CITY OF WILLIAMSBURG,

AND PARISH OF BRUTON.

FORMERLY OF HUNGARS PARISH ON THE

EASTERN SHORE

OF VIRGINIA, AND COUNTY OF NORTHAMPTON,

AGED 71 YEARS, AND YET LIVED BUT SEVEN YEARS,

WHICH WAS THE SPACE OF TIME HE KEPT

A BACHELOR'S HOME AT ARLINGTON,

ON THE EASTERN SHORE OF VIRGINIA

In this memorial, the decedent ignores the thirty-four years of merry widower-hood that he enjoyed after Frances died.

Through thick and thin, the husbands of the Parke sisters maintained their friendship through the years; perhaps their marital hardships drew them together. Both of them survived their spouses to enjoy over a quarter century more of life. Frances (her 1714 agreement of amity with Custis having been in effect for only a few months) died in 1715 of smallpox; the same all-prevalent disease claimed Lucy in London a year later.

Frances had always wanted to live amid the gaieties of Williamsburg rather than in the isolation of Arlington, but as long as she was John Custis's wife he refused to consider the idea. After her death, however, he built a large house on Francis Street and became a regular participant in the town's social life. The Governor's Palace was completed long before his death in 1749, and the round of receptions, concerts, and balls at the time of the spring and fall court sessions and Assembly meetings crowded the town to bursting with gentry from far and wide. A variety of taverns offered the men pleasant afternoons with a bottle of good claret, conversation with professors from the college on classics with which most were familiar, and the opportunity to share letters from England about prices on the London market and political affairs.

While a hostess would have been a convenient asset for entertaining, Custis never remarried.* Byrd, who had advised such a course, himself returned from London married to the widow of a merchant there. He had written Custis: "The match in the world that would most delight me, would be betwixt you and some charming nymph, that might by her fine qualities reconcile you to the sex." But Custis would have none of it; he declared himself "holding to that blessed resolution of abhoring Captivity; if it went hard with me when young, it must bee intolerable otherwise."[16]

---

*By one of his slaves, Custis had a son, Jack, to whom he was exceptionally devoted in comparison with his children by Fanny. In his last years his intimacy with the wife of one of Williamsburg's tavernkeepers was accompanied by gifts of family property, some of which his heirs demanded back upon his death.

Chapter 15

Island Governor

By the spring of 1706 Parke had tarried a year in London without receiving a hint of any alternative post. His departure for the West Indies could hardly be longer deferred. The paint was long dry on the portraits of himself that he had commissioned, and another man was in the parliamentary seat he had sought. Yet he took his appointment as governor of the Leewards almost as an affront.

Whitehall, by contrast, took a positive view of the Caribbean Islands. As Spain's power waned, the major nations of Europe had taken possession of these outcropping volcano tops that formerly had rimmed a private sea. Even during the Age of Discovery, when the Pope had drawn his Line of Demarcation dividing the new-found lands between Spain and Portugal, pockets of illicit exchange, peopled by traders from other countries, had appeared in convenient bays on coastlines too long to be effectively controlled by a single occupier. Now that Spain's primacy had passed, England and the Continental powers engaged in a flagrant rivalry. All saw the islands as stepping stones to a wider occupation of western territory, and as rich sources of such hitherto unknown or scarce products as tobacco and sugar.

The European nations attacked each other's colonies during their continental wars; even in intervals of European peace the colonies attacked each other, in conformity with the recognized doctrine: "No Peace Beyond the Line," that is, the Pope's Line of Demarcation.

So when Parke arrived a series of European flags—Spanish, Dutch, Danish, English, and French—fluttered in irregular order along the island chain. Until the conclusion of the Dutch-English wars of the seventeenth century, the Dutch had been the major enterpreneurs of trade in the islands. Now, except for a few tiny islets far to the south, the Dutch and the Danes held territory only in the Virgin Islands, where the chain just east of the large, Spanish-ruled island of Puerto Rico begins.

Next came the area of Parke's responsibility, the Leewards. On the northernmost island of any size in this group, St. Kitts, French and English settlements dating from independent arrivals in the early 1630s coexisted in uneasy occupation. The chief islands of the Leewards, south of St. Kitts, were Nevis and Antigua. Parke's territory ended with Montserrat.

To the south, the Windward group presented a mixed sequence: Guadeloupe and Marie Galante were French; Dominica was English; Martinique was French; then came a scattering of Danish and English small holdings down to Tobago, taken over from the Dutch by the English, and Trinidad, just off the South American coast. Barbados, the eastern outpost of the chain, was English too.

When these islands first began to be claimed, numerous promotional pamphlets described them as a tropical paradise, an earthly Eden, to be had for the taking by alert settlers. In England, where the elimination of the monasteries and the enclosure of formerly arable acres to increase pastures for sheep and cattle had set loose a large homeless and unemployed population, settlement overseas was vigorously urged by such publications as "A Plain Pathway to Plantations" by Richard Eburne, who addressed it to a group of West of England bishops:

> Considering, Right Honorable, and not without grief of mind and sorrow of heart viewing, the great misery and encumbrance of this our goodly country . . . by reason of the excessive multitude of people which therein at this present do swarm and

superabound, the many fair opportunities which God in his gracious providence ... at this instant doth offer unto it ... that he might stir and encourage them, especially the common and meaner sort of them, as whom chiefly and most of all it doth concern, to make better use of these fair ... opportunities.[1]

Like any piece of promotional literature, the story told by such an advisor was incomplete; it contained only very passing mention of the afflictions that European settlers encountered, some of them every day and every year. It is true that cleared acres were heavily fruitful, the waters abounded in fish, and the pastures were green year round. But there was more. When settlers of longer standing referred to new arrivals as "unseasoned" they meant that their capacity to sustain life in a tropical climate remained to be proved.

All year long, the unaccustomed heat was inescapable: droughts were frequent, prolonged and severe. The mean sea level temperature in these islands ranges from seventy-seven to eighty-two degrees; summer highs reach eighty-seven and winter lows drop only to seventy-five. By contrast, the English mean temperature is fifty degrees; London summers seem hot at sixty-four.

Furthermore, the semitropical heat to which Englishmen were entirely unaccustomed swirled up hurricane winds that slashed across the sea at velocities none of the settlers had previously witnessed. Tropical storms that made a direct passage across an island left only a scattering of whatever people and animals, crops and buildings lay in their paths. A local jingle ran: "June, too soon; July, stand by; August, you must; September, remember; October, all over."

The islands' original vegetation abounded with snakes and insects: the little flycatcher, a tiny lizard that scampered over dinner tables catching insects, was harmless, but out-of-doors, boas and the deadly fer-de-lance were not. Among smaller creatures, scorpions and tarantulas were only slightly less numerous than the harmless centipede.

And there was an unrecognized archenemy among prevalent insects: the anopheles mosquito whose bite transmitted malaria to hundreds or even thousands every year, weakening their resistance to every other disease. The yellow fever brought in on the ships was another dreaded competitor in annual mortality: it was normal for soldiers in regiments posted to the islands to be carried off by this scourge at a rate of 40 percent a year.

In addition to the dangers and casualties due to climate and environment, the later years of the seventeenth century were disturbed by a major economic transition that materially changed the islands' social structure. Initially, tobacco had been the immigrants' staple crop, on which they were almost totally reliant for their livelihood; it was so generally grown as to be usable as a medium of exchange. On relatively small individually owned tracts, it was cultivated by a yeomanry exclusively composed of family labor; or with a small number of the persons who emigrated under indenture and on arrival hired out for a period of years to repay their passage money; or, sometimes, with a few slaves.

But tobacco crops varied, and with them the prices they brought on English markets. In years of drought, prices would be high, but few people would have enough to sell to earn their living. When crops were very good, a glutted market would not yield an adequate return. And, although a reliable market existed for indigo because of its use as a dye, it was regarded as a secondary crop.

So in all of the islands producers turned to sugar. Like any one-crop system, this one also had its price problems, though the overseas market was larger than that for tobacco. Moreover, its efficient cultivation changed its producers' lives. Growing sugar on small holdings with settler labor was far less economic than planting large acreages and importing increasing numbers of African slaves. The quantity of sugar processed in the settlements doubled between the last decade of the old century and the first decade of the new. The revolution in production induced a social revolution: the white settler population declined and was replaced by substantial numbers of absentee plantation owners, while both the black population and the fear of slave uprisings increased. On the island of Antigua, between 1688 and 1706, the number of taxable land-owners fell from 53 to 36; the number of slaveholders rose from 16 to 30; and the number of slaves almost quadrupled, from 332 to 1150.[2]

The accompanying dislocation among the white population caused a turbulence that added to the usual ungovernability of a society on a new frontier and led to the passage of such laws as this:

> Whereas slaves are, for the brutishness of their natures, no otherwise valued or esteemed among us than as goods and chattels, therefore our prudent neighbours, as Barbados, etc., have thought fit to make laws to prevent the penalty and forfeiture in case of killing a negro, be it enacted that if any person ... shall in the deserved correction ... of his slave ... accidentally happen to kill such slave ... that the aforesaid owner ... shall not be liable ... to any penalty or forfeiture whatsoever ... provided always that if any person ... shall maliciously and wilfully kill or destroy ... any slave ... the aforesaid person ... shall forfeit and pay ... the full sum of ten pounds current money.[3]

Parke's ship dropped anchor at Antigua on July 14, 1706. As he repeatedly delayed his departure for the Islands, the officials on duty governing in his stead had grown restive. Lieutenant Governor Johnson, commander of the regiment assigned to the Leeward Islands, sighed, "I heartily wish for Col. Parke's arrival for I have such ill-natured and troublesome people to deal with, that I am already weary of my command."[4] His term of office was indeed brief: he took over when Parke's appointment was announced in 1705, and he was shot dead by a councilman of St. Kitts not long before Parke's arrival. When Parke finally appeared, there was a decided twang of reproach in greetings that assured him he had been greatly missed.

He took up the governorship in the middle of a very bad year. In March the French had attacked the English islands. With five ships of the line and a score of local vessels, they first landed on St. Kitts, where they failed to take the fort; but they had burned a number of English plantations before they received word that an English fleet was on the way. They then moved over to Nevis, taking some 300 slaves with them. Many of the settlers there fled to the mountains, but some were forced to capitulate. At first, they were kept on the island as prisoners, required to find French prisoners to exchange for their own liberty. By a second capitulation in early April, they agreed to send a certain number of their slaves, or their value in money, to Martinique within six months. The total operation netted the French between 3,000 and 4,000 slaves; the damage they did was so severe that Parliament was persuaded to vote £103,000 toward repairs.

At the same time, the annual epidemics in the Islands were exceptionally virulent. After Parke arrived, a rumor circulated that the two most dreaded of the French corsairs, de Chevennes and d'Iberville, were planning a raid. The rumor proved false only because of d'Iberville's death and the grim total of deaths among their sailors camped on Hispaniola. Half of the citizens of Nevis died from yellow fever during the summer of 1706.

On arrival, Parke's own entourage had numbered twenty-six. Five had gone back to England forthwith; of the twenty-one remaining, seventeen were dead by the time the epidemics were over. Describing his own seasoning, Parke wrote:

> I myself have had the Plague; the Pestilence and bloody flux, and have been out of my bed but 4 days of a malignant feaver; I am so weak I can hardly write. . . . Could I have foreseen what I was to suffer, and how little it was possible for me to gett, I wou'd never have come over.[5]

Parke had been disgruntled when he left London, and was prepared to be further disgruntled on arrival. The colony was disgruntled too. While the French had been dispossessed of their winnings on St. Kitts, the wrangling over plantation titles, property damage, missing slaves, etc., was far from over. Destruction of English fortifications had left the islands in a very poor position for defense, and nothing had been done to remedy the situation.

By the end of August, Parke was thoroughly disillusioned: "If I have my brains knokt out, the Queen must send some other unfortunate Divel here to be roasted in the sun, without the prospect of getting anything." By the end of October he was bewailing the current high prices: "Everything is so dear, I can hardly live upon my Incomb: and yet I never lived worse in all my life."[6]

And in the midst of these ravages of the natural climate, some of Parke's early actions worsened the political climate that awaited him as governor. He was quite possibly aware that Whitehall's decision to make him governor had been taken against the advice of the Lords of Trade, and against the wishes of his former patron, Lord Peterborough, who had regained his influence with Queen Anne. The men in charge of the colonies had preferred a competing candidate, Christopher Codrington.

The Codringtons had been in the islands since 1669, when King Charles II granted the islet of Barbuda, a few miles northeast of St. Kitts, to two brothers. One of them, Christopher, and his namesake son had between them served as the governor of the Leeward Islands for nearly fifteen years, from 1689 to 1703. In 1702, after England and France became chief actors in the War of the Spanish Succession, the French raided the English settlement on St. Kitts. Codrington's ejection of the intruders had so gratified the English landholders that the community had granted him a 763-acre plantation there in recognition of his services. But he had followed this exploit by participation in Admiral Sir Hoveden Walker's failed attack on the French island of Guadeloupe; during the recriminations that followed he had requested, and received, Queen Anne's permission to resign his governorship. Yet when Codrington requested to be reappointed after the appointee sent out from London died within

Christopher Codrington (1668–1710), governor of Leeward Islands 1697–1703, by Sir James Thornhill.—*Warden and Fellows of All Souls College, Oxford; courtesy of Sir Simon Codrington*

Caribbean hurricane. Engraving of unknown origin.
—*Folger Shakespeare Library*

the year, his petition was denied. That left Parke in the position of arriving to occupy Codrington's former place, and to face the experienced opposition of Codrington's powerful supporters.

Codrington's presence would have caused difficulties for any governor, but Parke handled it in a fashion that made matters worse. Parke's instructions, like those of any new governor, contained some problems for his first attention. One of these concerned the Codringtons.

Christopher, Sr., when governor (he died in 1698) had seized a vessel, charging the owner with engaging in illegal trade. The Admiralty Court in Antigua had dismissed the charge, but Codrington had overridden its verdict and confiscated ship and cargo. The outraged owner appealed the case to the High Court of Admiralty in London, which sustained the Antigua Court's ruling and required

Codrington to reimburse the owner; he died before doing so. Parke promptly pursued the matter.

The younger Codrington's irritation was the greater because he had just, at considerable expense, managed to extract from Her Majesty's treasury payment for four years of unpaid salary due his late father. He took the ship case back to London again, where a retrial in the islands was ordered. None occurred. Parke accurately observed that justice is difficult to obtain in a location where inter-marriage among the substantial families means that everyone who matters is everyone else's cousin.

He continued to harass Codrington under one of his general instructions that required him to check the authorization by which subordinate officers were holding their posts. The provision was not intended to become a review of land titles, many of which, to properties taken up at the time of first settlement, were vague, lost, or contradictory. Parke made a major misstep when he demanded that Codrington justify his control of Barbuda Island. Codrington was well able to produce all the necessary documents—from the family's original royal grant down to a ninety-nine year lease from Governor Johnson dated June 5, 1705.

Parke's third attack was aimed at the 763-acre plantation given the younger Christopher in appreciation of his liberation of St. Kitts. Codrington was then living at Betty's Hope, his plantation on Antigua. On the grounds that large, absentee ownership was generally agreed to be undesirable, Parke revoked the St. Kitts grant, depriving Codrington not only of his land but also of his investment in slaves, buildings, and equipment for its cultivation.

From then on, the relationship between the two men was one of opposition every step of the way. Both sent frequent complaints to London. By September, Codrington was writing to his old friend the Earl of Orrery (he also sent letters to Peterborough, Sunderland, and the ever-alert Blathwayt, now head of the customs service), expostulating that "It is impossible for me to live with our brute of a General —he is a perfect frenzy of avarice."[7] Before too long, Codrington departed in high dudgeon for Barbados, where the family had long owned land, and where, in Parke's view, he spent the rest of his life undermining Parke's authority. When he died in the spring of 1710, he was working with the group of Barbadians who quit the islands to found the port of Beaufort in South Carolina. His will established two educational institutions, Codrington College, on his Barbados estate, and Codrington Library at All Souls College, Oxford.

In the year 1707, the year when the union of England and Scotland was consummated, military matters claimed Parke's chief attention. In its early months he horrified Whitehall with a proposal whose repercussions might have been very damaging indeed had news of it got out.

From the time of his Williamsburg clashes with Commissary Blair to his displacement by Lord Orkney as the choice for the governorship of Virginia, Parke had detested the Scots. In January 1707 he asked Secretary of State Hedges to:

> Send me over tenn thousand Scotch with otemeal enough to keep them for 3 or 4 months . . . [he would use them to take Martinique from the French, or Puerto Rico from the Spanish]. Lett us try our ffortune, if wee take it, we will have the plunder, the Scotch shall have the Land, in time the warm sun will exhale all those crudeties that makes them so troublesom, and 'tis not impossible but it may have the effect to make them of a more sociable Religion; if we have not success if you chuse out those that are so zealous to maintain the Kerke and against the Union: if I get them all knock'd on the head, I am off the openion the English Nation will be no great loosers by it.[8]

He wrote in a similar vein to the Council of Trade and Plantations, ending: "P.S. If the Queen will not spare English troops, send us 10,000 Scotch . . . If they chuse out all zealous kirkmen, I promise they shall never trouble the Queen's affairs more; if they do not take Martineque, I will gett them disposed off, and I think that will be some service."[9]

When this proposal reached him, Lord Sunderland, in fury, snapped back: "I am to tell you H.M. does totally reject your proposal of sending 10,000 Scots. . . . H.M. looks upon them as good subjects and good Christians, too good to be knock't on the head upon so wild a project."[10]

The extent to which official patience with Parke was wearing thin is evidenced by the quizzical advice sent to Marlborough by Godolphin that midsummer. Godolphin had received a letter from Parke, which stated that "The Duke promised me the Government of Virginia at ye battle of Blenheim, but for some reasons of State, that was given to my Ld. Orkney, and this given to me wth a promise ye sallery should be the same wich is 2000 1. ster. the year. I find myselfe mistaken, and at this distance forgot." Apparently, at the same time Parke had sent a letter directly to Marlborough, which looked identical from the outside. Godolphin forwarded his letter to the Duke with the suggestion: "If it bee like mine within, I should advise you not to give yourself the trouble of opening it till you are at full leisure."[11]

In the latter part of the year, however, prospects of a new French invasion were sufficiently threatening to distract the settlers from their local quarrels, and Parke's actions, even though his complaints continued, were decisive enough to gain him credit in London. He was seeing to the repair of defenses that had been allowed to remain in ruins after the hostilities that preceded his arrival; and he was keeping in touch with other governors in a watch that revealed the potential seriousness of an imminent threat. The dimensions of French preparations appear in the intelligence that he forwarded in mid-November to two governors of larger islands south and west of his province. One of them, Col. Thomas Handasyde, head of Her Majesty's forces and governor of Jamaica, he had come to know in the Blenheim campaign. To him, he dispatched a sloop carrying a secret report brought back from French Martinique by an informant who had left that island under cover of darkness on the night of November 10. The report was an eyewitness account of the arrival of French warships on their way to rendezvous with others at the island of Tobago:

Antigua November ye 18th 1707

On Wednesday the eleventh Instant arrived at Martinique Monsr Du Cass with ten men of war and severall large privateers with land forces on board, eight of them are Ships from Seventy to eighty Six Guns, they expect eighteen more.

This Account is brought me by a Gentleman I sent up in a fflagg of Truce, that knows Monsr Du Casse and saw him, who got away the same night. I have sent Advice of this to Barbados, and have hired this sloop to Carry the Same Account to your Excellency. I thought it of so great Consequence to give you timely Notice of it, for though I shall neglect nothing in my Power to put the Islands under my Care into the best posture of Defence they are capable of, yet I can't but think this too great a force to be sent out to Attack these Islands. I believe their Design is either for Barbados, or Jamaica or Curasao, perhaps I may receive a Visitt as they pass by. I have obliged the Master to touch at Curasao to give their Governor the Same Notice.

You had had the News sooner, but 'twas the 16th at night (the sloop meeting with Calms) before I had it, then I called a Councill and Assembly, and desired them to send a Sloop with Advice to you at the publick Charge, wch. they refused, because on the like Occasion before I came to the Government, they sent to your Island an Advice Boat and your Assembly Refused to pay the Charge, notwithstanding which, I thought the Queen's Interest so much concerned that Liberty to Carry twenty-five pipes of wine only as Ballast for the Sloop, and if your Assembly will not pay it, I must. I am

S^r
Your Excell^cys
Most humble Servant
Daniell Parke [12]

The Mr. Chester who carried this message was the area chief of the Royal African Company and one of the ranking residents of Antigua. His smuggling skills were well known, and he would well understand how to convert the considerable amount of wine mentioned by Parke as ballast into untaxed sales to thirsty gentlemen on the island of Jamaica.

Just as Chester was departing, an English warship, the *Greenwich*, appeared off St. Johns. Colonel Codrington was aboard, and on behalf of the warship's captain, he came ashore to inform Parke of the captain's desire to moor there. But Parke persuaded the captain to sail back to Barbados at once, taking with him a duplicate of his letter to Colonel Handasyde, thus warning each of the major islands east and west of Tobago of the fleet forming up there.

The *Greenwich* must have been a good sailer, for Mitford Crowe, the Barbadian governor, received the word in a very short time. On November 25 he held a meeting of his council to "consider what measures might be necessary to be taken at this juncture." Magazines were to be checked, commissions distributed, forts and fortifications put in order; the colonels of the several regiments were to inform the governor of their supplies of arms, first having inspected their condition, etc., etc. The public records were also to be removed from the capital to the safety of a residence named Moonshine Hall.[13]

In reporting the deficiencies of his own military situation after reviewing the single regiment at his disposal Parke listed absenteeism among his officers, indifferent quality in their men, lack of an engineer, and lack of munitions. He also repeated his earlier dissatisfaction with his post: "I hope if I deserve well, the Queen will give me something better, for I can never get any thing here."[14]

Whether or not French intelligence regarding the degree of preparation that resulted from Parke's dispatches to other governors caused the French to desist from plans for a strike at the English holdings, none took place at this time. In the resulting leisure, Parke and his settlers resumed their domestic quarrels.

By March 1708, Parke's restlessness had led him to enhance the enmity of Secretary of State Sutherland by declaring that: "When I brought the Queen the good news, I had her royal word that she would take care of my ffortune: I think Her Majesty cannot do it worse, if she does it at all."[15] On receipt of this announcement, Sunderland's temper flared again: "I am very sorry to hear of any misunderstanding between you and Col. Codrington, or any one else, but hope your own prudence and temper will overcome those difficultys. I know of no better way to secure you in your post than by ffaithful and diligent discharge of your trust."[16]

New unrest among the settlers occurred when Parke, on his own initiative, added new members to the council. The Lords of Trade accepted his reason for doing so when he declared that a quorum was otherwise frequently unobtainable: a number of those on the list he had been given when commissioned were either dead, bedridden, gone to England, or unwilling to take the oath; and at the date of any given meeting, one or two others were apt to be off the island.

By this time, council meetings were held in the imposing Government House that Parke had built at St. John's on Antigua to provide a suitable meeting place for both the council and the interisland assembly. The settlers held its scale to be extravagant, and the people of Nevis had been antagonized when he moved guns and troops from that island to guard the new building. Within its walls, increasingly substantial differences began to be argued. Assembly members advanced claims of additional powers that went so far as to assert that their speaker, rather than the governor, had the right of legislative veto. When Parke denied this, the members cut off payment of the 100,000 pounds of tobacco they had voted on his arrival for his house rent.

Yet from first to last, the basic public cause of ill will among the citizens was Parke's effort to enforce the Acts of Trade. Such enforcement was a prime part of a governor's function: he was bonded for £2,000 to see that these acts were carried out; at the same time he was entitled to a third of the value of proven condemnations under them. When Parke tried using writs of assistance to get aid in his searches and seizures, he had great difficulty finding anyone willing to assist him. When he used soldiers for such tasks, resistance doubled. When he brought cases to court, the judges rather regularly found for the defendants. At the same time, the Board of Trade was not wholly sure that Parke was not himself guilty of illicit transactions: he had admitted to offshore trading to obtain claret for his own table.

Montserrat continued to be a favored rendezvous where sugar could be exchanged for foreign products without payment of either the import duties on such goods or the 4½ percent export tax on sugar and other agricultural commodities traded for them. This island had a considerable Irish population that felt small obligation to England. They had little interest in paying an export tax the proceeds of which would be used for the English colony's government salaries and other costs.

Almost all planters smuggled. Edward Chester's operations were as large in volume as he was clever in logistics.* As Chester and others grew more dissatisfied with Parke, they sent one William Nevine to London with a collection of charges against him and £1,000 to encourage Lord Peterborough to effect his recall.

In the autumn of 1708 there were riots in the islands, and Parke became sufficiently alarmed to write to Marlborough: "I hope your Grace will not lett me be removed."[17] The year 1709 was worse. Parke received a copy of Nevine's extended charges against him, and news that the settlers had increased to £5,000 their fund to press the charges through. Micajah Perry was assiduously collecting affidavits in Parke's favor to exhibit to the Lords of Trade, but other London merchants were alleged to have joined the plaintiffs. Parke felt that the seriousness of the situation warranted a further plea for help from Marlborough. The main thrust of a long letter is his entreaty for the Duke to use his influence with Godolphin:

---

*Chester taunted Parke with the information that his salary was twice the governor's.

Slaves at work making cassava flour and sorting tobacco. From du Terte, *Histoire générale des Antilles.—William L. Clements Library, University of Michigan*

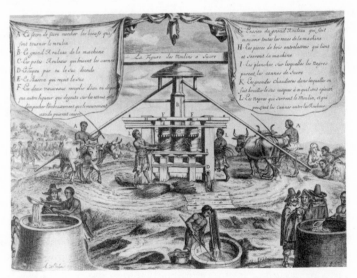

Seventeenth-century sugar mill in operation. From Charles de Rochefort, *Histoire naturelle et morale des îles Antilles de l'Amérique* (1665).*—Library Company of Philadelphia*

My Lord Treasurer by being in Councill has I hope heard my Defence to what I have been Charged with and the more malice appears against me so much the better title shall I have to your Grace's Favour and Protection while I do nothing to deserve the Contrary as I hope my Lord Treasurer thinks I have not if you'l Condescend to talke of it to him.[18]

Since the beginning of the year, news of Parke, of varying degrees of accuracy, had begun to be received in Virginia, where the ciphered pages of William Byrd's diary had by now suggested that "father Parke" had apparently forgotten about the younger generation of his Old Dominion family. A sequence of reports arrived in April. The first, dated April 1, stating "that my father Parke was killed . . . which God grant may not be true" was dismissed as an April fool's message when a week later John Custis picked up the word that Parke "instead of being killed was married to his housekeeper." Byrd rejected this information as being the "more improbable" of the two accounts. Ten days later, a Mr. Connor "told me his sloop came in the last of March from Barbados, and brings word that the king of France was dead, and that my father Parke was well and not married."[19]

In early September, Parke himself wrote that all was well, but in mid-October another letter from him informed the family that he "had like to have been assassinated by a negro hired for the purpose who shot at him and broke his arm."[20]

This was true. On September 5, an ambush had been set up by men impatient of London's deliberate speed in responding to their petitions. It was only because Parke's nervously sensitive horse had suddenly sidestepped on reaching the ambush that the bullet missed the governor's body and went through his sleeve. Feeling had clearly risen toward a climax; it was improbable that violence would be long deferred.

Chapter 16

Murder in Midmorning

In 1710, drought and disease decimated crops and populations in the Lesser Antilles. Parke reported that among his soldiers "every fifth or sixth man was dead of a fever and sore throat." Unrest spread along the entire island chain. In January, Parke took the precaution of making a will.

When the economic crisis forced the governor to call a meeting of the Leeward Islands legislature in order to obtain emergency funds, a dispute over who had the right to appoint the Assembly's clerk —the members or the governor—broke the session up in a riot. On June 10, in Virginia, Byrd received a visit from a member of the Bland family "who came from Williamsburg and told us that Col. Parke was recalled from his Governorship." On August 15, an ambiguous letter from Parke partially denied this: he "told us he was going to England but was not put out and though he was dismissed he should not be put out if he could justify himself from the accusation against him."[1]

In fact, Nevine had returned from England, bringing an order from Lord Sunderland that required Parke to come home with the autumn fleet to stand trial before the Queen. Declaring that he had not been informed of the main charges against him until the day before the fleet sailed, Parke did not comply. On September 9, he sent a 104-page refutation of the complaints against him.[2] But on September 29, after hearing that Sunderland had been replaced by

Lord Dartmouth as secretary of state, he took heart and promised to be in London by Christmas.

He was still toying with the idea that a successful parliamentary candidacy could free him from his governorship. On November 11, he was referring to his assets in England—a clear estate of £550 a year in Hampshire and another in Middlesex—and noting "I will be home time enough to be chosen into the House, if the Parliament is not dissolved until after this season."[3]

In the islands, his prospects were grim. Over recent months, the planters had acquired a new cause for resentment. During the last years of Parke's tenure, not all of the settler's grievances had been related to public affairs. The wrath that inflamed his official opposition was also fed by the extent to which the governor had been trifling with other men's wives and daughters. Although the settlers' own morals were those of a frontier town, they expected, and indeed enforced, a certain mutual respect of turf. Codrington had had an illegitimate son while governor, but he had been discreet about it.

It was quite otherwise when Catharine, wife of Edward Chester, was delivered of a daughter. Parke's public acceptance of paternity included endowing the baby with the name Lucy, the same as his mother and one of his legitimate daughters in Virginia. So when Chester swore that he "would gladly lie seven years in Hell to be avenged," no one thought he was referring solely to Parke's interference with his smuggling ventures.

In listing alleged wrongs done to Edward Chester, a pamphlet published in London in 1713, "Some Instances of the Oppression and Male Administration of Col. PARKE, late Governor of the Leeward Islands," states the main grievances of the islanders on both public and private account. On the public score, the author stresses Parke's persecution of Chester under the Acts of Trade: "by making frequent and groundless seizures of his Goods, and by this Means got into his Possession a considerable Part of Mr. Chester's Estate." Parke's searches and seizures are said to have taken him into Chester's house "at unseasonable Times, and in different Disguises." When Chester, by chance, caught him "skulking behind the Door of a Room adjoining to Mrs. Chester's bed-chamber," Parke drew his sword and offered to fight. Chester was unarmed, and undressed to his shirt. Whistling up two attending soldiers for support, Parke ended the incident by threatening to ruin Chester if he did not "take in his Wife again, whom he had turned out of doors upon this Occasion."[4]

Parke did not leave the islands in time to be back in London by Christmas. A new French threat brought warships to Martinique, forcing him to call an Assembly session in December to vote for arms and make plans for defense, even though tensions between himself and the Assembly were stretched to the snapping point.

On December 5, just before the session was scheduled to open, Assembly members forced themselves into Government House where Parke was sitting in Council and attempted to hand him a petition announcing that they were "withdrawing our obedience from you as Chief Governor." He refused to receive it and prorogued the session for two days, during which time he holed up in the building, stationing soldiers at the windows and manning a few artillery pieces outside. During this interval, Assembly members and settlers consulted with each other. Parke offered to yield on a number of points, but on nothing related to his commission.

The foreseeable explosion occurred on the morning of December 7. Legislators and militia crowded into one of the two meadows adjacent to Government House, the general citizenry into the other. Then, advancing to the door, they attempted to present a petition, "The Address to Governor Parke sent from the Inhabitants with Arms," asking the governor to withdraw to a retired position, perhaps to Nevis, while the Council and Assembly agreed on measures of defense. He refused, replying that he was the Queen's representative and so long as he had breath in his body would not yield to force. According to one account, he then ordered one of the cannon outside to be fired into the crowd.

The settlers forced their way indoors. Shortly, shots were exchanged. Parke killed Captain Piggott, leader of the citizen contin-

Daniel Parke II. Engraving by George Vertue (1684–1756), after Kneller's portrait. Printed on the front page of George French, *History of Col. Parke's Administration*, a 1717 pamphlet in defense of the governor.
—*Virginia Historical Society*

gent, one of whose partisans shot, though he did not kill, Michael Ayon, a Parke supporter. A bullet penetrated Parke's thigh and broke the bone.

But, though depositions and affidavits were promptly taken, there is little certainty about what else actually occurred on that bloody forenoon. The statements of eyewitnesses, each firmly declaring that what he or she affirmed was true, present irreconcilable observations. There is agreement that following the shooting indoors Parke was carried out of Government House and laid in the street; and that thereafter he was removed to a nearby house, where he died some two hours later with a physician in attendance. But there agreement ends. What happened at Government House when the riot started, and during the interval when Parke was carried to the street, are described so variously that reconciliation of the accounts is impossible.

Some participants were ready to swear that prior to being carried outside, Parke was beaten with musket butts until his back was broken. Those who held to this scenario went on to say that while indoors he was stripped naked, with the rioters sharing the clothes as they took them off. (The locket given him by the Queen was subsequently exhibited as a prize trophy by a rioter alternatively described as a butcher or a farrier; he could have been both.)

The Government House that Parke had built at public expense was in the opinion of many on a scale far in excess of island requirements. Its entrance was approached by an imposing flight of stone steps such as one might admire before a building of some importance in London. When, seizing him by an arm and his uninjured leg, the crowd dragged him out into the street, the rioters viewed and heard with relish the bumping of his head from one step to the next all the way down: all the accounts refer to it, though there is no estimate of how much this treatment contributed to his death. Once in the street he was laid down in the scorching sun, out of whose heat he begged to be removed. A woman who tried to bring him water was threatened "to have a Sword in her Guts"; a man "went to him when he was dyeing and spitt in his face." Only after that sequence of torment was he taken to the adjacent dwelling.[5] Yet testimony equally firmly held, but opposite in content, states that such accounts are "sufficiently confuted by the Answer of Doctor *Gouffe Bonnine*, upon Oath to the Interragatories exhilted to him at *Antegia* in Council, who was the Chyurgion that attended upon the Governor, and declares that he came out of the House at the same time that the Governor was carried out, and that he neither saw nor knew that any Person had beat, wounded, bruised or dragged him. That he went to the House to which the Governor was carryed, and tarried with him till his Death."[6]

Others besides the doctor affirmed that nothing of this sort happened, pointing out that the back-breaking could not have occurred, because during his last hours Parke was very "uneasy," constantly changing his position, which would have been impossible with a broken back. The woman who prepared Parke's body for burial stated under oath that far from being rasped by gravel, except for the bullet hole in his thigh, his skin was unblemished.

After its dying quarry had disappeared into the neighboring house, the crowd was momentarily at a loss, but then turned to looting. It subjected Government House to a thorough pillage—of its silver, china, glass, furnishings, and private papers. The papers would have been better off left where they were: their perusal in local homes incited additional outrage by revealing a disconcerting number of hitherto unsuspected liaisons between Parke and feminine members of their readers' families.

Perhaps because of the wrath that accompanied these new findings, a considerable number of the depositions describe the extent of Parke's rake's progress, naming specific cases. The derogation of Parke's feminine associates had a double usefulness: it served to disparage the value of their testimony about the riot. Elizabeth Sweegle was described not only as an "abandoned Strumpet, and particularly to Col. Parke," but as having frankly declared that she would "leave not only Father and Mother, but also her Savior to follow him."

Elinor Martin was branded as "having been a known assistant to him in his lewdness, and, as was commonly reported in Antegoa, in debauching her own daughter."

Among those most vigorously castigated was Lucia French, the wife of George French, one of Parke's longtime cronies. She was included in a group of "Persons noted for their lewd and profligate lives, and infamous Characters . . . having been publicly whipt for her enormous crimes." French himself had been inside the house during the fracas there; he testified that when "lying in the gore of some wounds he had before received," he was shot in the mouth; but "to the great wonder and surprise of all," he recovered. He became Parke's staunch defender as author of the poignant final pamphlet on the murder, *The History of Colonel Parke's Government of the Lee-ward Islands*, published in London in 1717.* After a chronology that follows the most lurid of the scenarios, ending as Parke is "drag'd naked on the coarse, gravelly, and stiff clayey Street, which rak'd the Skin from his Bones," French concludes:

Those Cruelties and Tortures force Tears from his Eyes and in this Condition he is left expiring . . . but makes no other Return, then these mild Expressions. "Gentlemen, if you have no Sense of Honour left, pray have some of Humanity." He gratefully owns the kindness of Friends, and prays God to reward those who stood by him on that Day . . . recommending his Soul to God and some pious Ejaculations, he pays the great Debt of Nature; and Death, less cruel than his Enemies, puts a Period to his Pains and Sufferings.

*French first published this by itself in pamphlet form as a version of what happened, then reprinted it as the first section of a beautifully leather-bound book, printed and sold by the booksellers of London and Westminster in 1717, dedicated to Marlborough, and with George Vertue's engraving of Kneller's portrait of Parke as its frontispiece. In this latter version, he included a section on what he regarded as the too-lenient attitude adopted by Lieutenant General Hamilton towards the rioting settlers after Parke's death. A second addition gave his own sympathetic view of the difficulties of Walter Douglas, the next man to be sent out from London as a governor. French's version of the circumstances of Parke's murder are given on pages 56–65 of his book.

Thus dy'd Col. Parke, whose brave End shews him sufficiently deserving the Commission which he bore, and by his triumphant Death, acquir'd an Honour to his Memory.

The rancor of the populace did not subside at nightfall. It effectively blocked all plans for a funeral, opposing Parke's burial in the churchyard. Several days of tropical heat went by before the opponents yielded. "They pulled down the very pew in which Parke usually sat," though warned that it had been erected from public funds "for all their generals." Over time, Government House disappeared, and eventually a church was built on the spot that once witnessed the obscenities of the murder.

Marlborough received a summary of the events of the murder early in March 1711, from an eyewitness's account which the duke's young relative, Major William Churchill, enclosed in a letter. This account, too, ended with a recognition of Parke's personal courage, declaring that he had had ample warnings from concerned islanders urging that since "the Queen had superceded him," he should leave. In reply, "he had put all his Affaires in a Posture and sent for the Minister and took the Sacrament, and behaved himself with a great deal of Bravery to the last, alledging that as the Queen had given him a Commission he would not part with it otherwise than with Sword and Pistol in hand."[7]

But by the time this letter reached Marlborough, the hero of Blenheim had been overwhelmed by troubles of his own.

Whatever the details may have been, it was undeniable that an English governor had been murdered in broad daylight by the subjects he had been sent to govern. But it was equally undeniable that, given the current political situation, in both London and Antigua, any attempt to investigate the murder and punish the murderers would be a dangerously delicate undertaking.

Chapter 17

Aftermath

IN the midst of domestic turmoil, London in 1710 had become a city of fallen pedestals, where yesterday's great men were great no more. In the whirlwind of such change, murder on a small, faraway island in the Caribbean, even that of a royal governor, was barely visible. England was in the midst of one of the cyclical changes that accompany constitutional party politics. In the shredding of the Morley-Freeman friendship, contrary to what Anne had written long ago, death had been preceded by politics. The year 1710 was the year when the green worm of envy, that for nearly a decade had been gnawing at the ties connecting Marlborough and Godolphin with the throne, severed the last threads. The High Tories were taking over the management of public affairs. During recent months the Queen's new confidante, Mrs. Masham, had moved closer and closer to the throne, and Sarah Churchill had been pushed away.

The Queen began to appoint new ministerial advisors. On August 8, 1710, Her Majesty dismissed Godolphin, informing Marlborough that his colleague's behavior being "not the same to me that it was formerly, made it impossible for me to let him keep the white staff any longer, and, therefore, I ordered him this morning to break it."[1] By the time of the 1710 riot in Antigua, Anne was turning on Sarah; and even though Marlborough, in mid-January 1711, besought her on behalf of his beloved, she insisted that her Keeper of the Privy Purse turn in her key.

High Tories replaced Moderate Tories and Whigs in the ministries, and the 1710 election brought the party a triumphant control of Parliament. The Duke of Ormond's exultation conveys the new mood:

> What Change, and what a Chagrin was it to some, and what Joy to others, when I arrived at *London* all were in an Emotion, the Duke of *Marlborough* was removed from every one of his employments, and the Duke of *Somerset* likewise.[2]

Within two years, Ormond occupied Marlborough's former place as commander-in-chief and captain general of the armed forces.

In Antigua, the Inter-Island Council, in acrimonious discussion, divided, with some of its members appealing to the Queen for punishment of the ringleaders while others urged her to regard them as champions of liberty against oppression. The former were in a decided minority.

Most islanders were enjoying a sense of accomplishment and impunity. Both General Hamilton and the new governor, Walter Douglas, after he arrived, counseled Whitehall against any attempt to punish the rioters. Their leaders were believed to have a large voting majority and certainly enjoyed very wide popular support. The citizen on St. Kitts who murdered the islands' military commander during the interval before Parke's arrival in 1706 was cleared by a jury and then elected to the Inter-Island Assembly. The riot had been a mass uprising. Few settlers had not participated; and all kinds of people had been present at the confrontation.

The Council minority, convinced that the riot had been an insurrection against Her Majesty's government, approved the advice sent to Whitehall by Andrew Boult, a friend of Parke, who warned that "the eyes of all the Collonys are on their Mother Kingdom, and how she will punish such an outrage." Nevertheless he recognized that though "the majority of Antigua have drank so deep of this gentleman's blood, they will find no person guilty of tasting it, and the most solemn trial there will be but eluding justice." Boult suggested reaching the islanders through their pride, declaring any person who, on the oath of two witnesses, had been a participant in the riot "for ever incapable of any post civil or military or of being members of the Council or Assembly, or officers of the Militia."[3]

Action in London was shortly complicated by the necessity of recalling Walter Douglas as governor. As the man who had been sent out to apprehend the murderers and restore order, he had taken certain measures in that direction; but he was also exhibiting an unacceptable rapacity in "getting" for his own use by extensive bribery. He was discovered to have converted into bullion the silver communion service sent out with him for the church in Antigua. Ironically enough, among all those who were guilty in one way or another, he was the only one called back to England to suffer a trial, conviction, fine, and a five-year prison sentence.

No royal decision on policy was evident until February 1712: On February 4, a proclamation was posted in Antigua appointing the twentieth as a day of fasting and atonement for Parke's murder. Two days later, the Queen signed a second proclamation in London; it granted a general pardon for participants in the uprising, explaining that Her Majesty was persuaded that "many of the offenders were drawne into the rebellion and murder by the subtle insinuations and by the influence of some of the chief advisers and promoters thereof, and not from any rancour of mind or disposition to our Government." At the same time, a warning was conveyed by the statement that "if any of the persons hereby meant or intended to have the benefit of this our gracious and free pardon shall presume to justifye the murder aforesaid, or shall assemble and meet together in order to obstruct justice or shall attempt like rebellious practices . . . they shall receive no benefitt . . . but be liable to prosecution."[4]

While London wavered in indecision, news of Parke's death was received in Virginia. On April 11, a letter from Barbados reached William Byrd, telling him "the sad news that my father Parke was shot through the head in the Leeward Islands. He told me no particulars because it was a melancholy subject. I told it my wife as gently as I could and it affected her very much but I comforted her as well as I could by telling her that his enemies killed him because he should not make their villainy appear in England."[5]

That September, the naturalist Mark Catesby of Williamsburg, himself familiar with the Caribbean islands from past residence there, assured Byrd that "Several of Colonel Parke's murderers were taken and some sent to London in irons"; he probably referred to the brief imprisonment of four men on the islands and two who went to England. No one was actually tried until June 1714, when a single suspect was brought before the Court of King's Bench, to be promptly released for lack of evidence.[6]

Meanwhile, Perry had probated the will that Parke had drawn in January 1710. Its main bequests were to three separate beneficiaries: his illegitimate daughter Lucy Chester in Antiqua; his illegitimate son Julius Caesar, now a seaman; and his legitimate offspring in Virginia. Three members of the Perry firm, Micajah and Richard Perry, and Thomas Lane, the family's longtime associate, were appointed executors for England and Virginia; Thomas Long, Caesar Rodney, and Major Sam Byam for the Islands. (Colonel Long died during 1710; Parke substituted Abraham Redwood in his place on the day before the riot.)

All of the legatees were bound by one requirement that Parke had taken over from his father's will: they must either bear the name of Parke or adopt it before qualifying for a bequest. Daniel II even increased his father's concern for the family name by stipulating that heirs also make use of the Parke arms, "of my Family of the County of Essex."*

At first glance, the bequest to a baby so young as to be yet unchristened (though Parke had said her name should be Lucy) seemed

---

*The Parkes to whom Daniel referred were a distantly related family of Gestingthorpe, Essex; at the time of the Visitation of Essex in 1634, their arms were described as "Azure an eagle displayed argent, gutty de sang, legged and beaked or."

clearcut. All of Parke's estate on the islands, land, houses, slaves, and receivable debts were to be hers, though if she died before age twenty-one, a life interest in it was to be enjoyed by her mother, on whose death the principal should go to the man whom Parke called his godson, Julius Caesar. (In any case, Julius Caesar was to receive £50 per annum for life.) Future wrangling developed from the fact that while the right of the heirs to receive debts owed to Parke is mentioned, their responsibility for debts owed by him is not. If an heir refused to adopt the Parke name, the bequest should go to the godson, and if he too refused, to Fanny's male heir, or if there were none, to the male heir of the legitimate Lucy.

The estate in England and Virginia was willed to Frances, the elder of his legitimate daughters, with its succession, if she had no son, to be the legitimate Lucy, Lucy Chester, Julius Caesar, and, in the case of failure of all such heirs, the poor of Whitchurch in Hampshire. Frances's sister Lucy was to have the £1,000 that was in actuality the more-than-five-years-late payment of the dowry that Parke had promised but never produced. As final items, Parke's sisters and their children were each to have £50 for mourning rings, and the English executors £20. Payment of the bequests, other than those in the Islands, were to be made by Frances from her receipts from the estate.

When Micajah Perry read the will, it destroyed his usual calm. In a letter to Byrd sent with a copy of the will he regrets all the work he did before Parke's recall—the "inexpressible trouble" of attempting the governor's vindication—and inquires of Byrd:

> What shall we say to such a man that would make his bastard children so easy to have all that he had mulk't together and was as ready money; and tye all his debts and legacys upon his estate in England and Virginia. We can't with patience reflect upon his unkindness.[7]

He specifically washes his hands of Julius Caesar:

And for Julius Caesar you must shift with him as well as you can: we resolve to have nothing to do with him; we have cast him off, he hath spent the colonel no small sum and had we followed the colonel's order, it would have been more, but let him go a bastard as he is, and see who will regard him. We think he is in prison still, and there shall be for us.[8]

Members of the Perry firm, as longtime managers of the Parkes' crop shipments to England and the purchases and investments from their sales, probably had a clearer idea than anyone else of the position of the estate, and they were well aware that a certain number of debts were outstanding. Micajah's calculations of Parke's borrowing shows that "Cousin Brown" (Mrs. Barry) was still alive and well, though possibly disgruntled: She and Parke's two younger sisters had been ill-advised enough to extend him currently unpaid loans of £500 each. Perry reports that as he writes the third sister, Mrs. Pepper, is about to descend on him, accompanied by her husband, to see if Parke's will can be construed to leave something for her sons. The Perry indebtedness totals are:

To Messrs. Perry—about all dry money*	£2,400
To Anne Humfreys	500
To Rebecca Goodart	500
To a mortgage on his estate at White Church & interest	2,230
To Mrs. Barry	500
To law charges not yet paid his sollicitor	120
To Sir James Hallott	30
	£6,280
To pay this is his estate at White Church which may be sold for	4,000
	£2,280

*Mostly cash.

To the queen's demand tho' not settled above   400

£2,680[9]

Regrettably, the Perry list displayed only the tip of the iceberg. As more and more obligations came in for Frances to meet from the English and Virginia properties, the Custises were forced to seek court permission to sell lands and slaves to pay them. Byrd, however, found the approaching alienation of valuable properties painful. He could never bear to see a fruitful acre lost to the family. He therefore suggested to the Custises a plan to hold onto the mill and the many plantations: he would take responsibility for the Parke debts in England and Virginia if they would make over to him the acres and slaves that would otherwise have to be sold.

When they approved, an agreement was drawn up. Its form shows that both Byrd and Custis were well aware of the importance of covering all possible contingencies in advance if an agreement of this order were to work smoothly between brothers-in-law. A memorandum accompanying the agreement stipulated that: some wild horses and a partly broken stallion at one of the plantations should not be included; Byrd should have land in Prince William County recently recovered by one H. G. Child from Parke's attorneys if he could secure it either by suit or agreement; debts due before Custis took over management of Parke's plantations should be paid by him and Byrd in equal shares, but all since then until the signing of the new agreement by Custis only; if any of the slaves should die before sunrise on the day the agreement is signed, their value should be accounted for.

Lest even this carefulness should not prevent a snag, Byrd wrote further notes to Custis as the day approached for signing:

As both of us mean uprightly in our bargain without any design of surprise, so I doubt not but we understand that my sister will confirm the sale of Whitchurch and the mony for which it was sold must go in part of payment of Col. Parkes debts. I understand it so, and I should be glad if you signifyd as much under your hand and my sister too so that our agreement may be as plain as possible.[10]

Byrd's awareness of possible difficulties with Frances is clear both from this and from a further note three days later:

To do take every thing to be upon honor between us, and tho the last article concerning all manner of effects in England woud secure me in the affair of Whitchurch, yet I was willing to clear up every doubt between us to avoid all shaddow of controversy. As to my sisters fears concerning the debts due to Col. Parke in Virginia, as they were no part of my thoughts when we made the articles, so I shoud never have claimd them.[11]

Yet in spite of all of Byrd's care, the agreement came very close to being left unsigned. His diary for April 19, 1712, says "My brother Custis came this morning before I got up to tell me that my sister was resolved not to agree to our bargain concerning the selling of the land and negroes. I was surprised at it but thought it only a strategem to prevail with her husband to live at Williamsburg. . . . I had a letter from her with many things very foolish in it."[12]

Two days later, however, while he and Dr. Cocke were discussing the Custis difficulty, "my brother Custis came in and told me my sister would acknowledge conveyances on some of the articles agreed between them . . . about 6 my wife came and let me know all was well at home, thank God. I waited on her to Queen's Creek where I could not disguise my resentment to my sister."[13]

But by April 25, everything had been straightened out:

I rose about 6 o'clock and my brother and sister Custis came about 7 to perfect the deed between us. There were several little quarrels between my brother and his wife, and my wife could not forbear siding with her sister. . . . However at last everything was agreed between us and we signed and sealed.

. . . About 11 I went to court and about 2 came in the women to acknowledge their deed in court.[14]

So the plan went into operation. But as London packet after London packet reached Virginia ports, or sloops arrived in coastal shipping down the American coast, they brought letters to Byrd with content similar to that from Mrs. Gertrude Schuyler van Courtlandt of New York, who wrote on January 29, 1713:

> I am heartily sorry to hear of the death of General Parkes which occasions my offering this trouble to you, but I am mightily pleased to hear that such an honest and worthy gentleman as yourself has been pleased to take upon you the sole management of his affairs. . . . I have sent you here in enclosed an account of pretty old standing. The particulars I have formerly sent your father in law. However it happened I never had no return, nor satisfaction made me to this day. But hopes now my just demands (considering your integrity) shall never give me the occassion of troubling you above this once.[15]

As time went on, outpayments in response to such bills made Byrd land poor. A man who on his death owned some 179,000 acres could only be called wealthy, but by 1719 he was writing his brother Custis that "If you knew how much money I have been forc't to pay on Col. Parks account here in England, more than appeard to be due when I made the contract with you, you would not think you had an ill bargain, tho you tarry a little longer for your tobacco debt."[16]

Over the next few years, Custis in his turn became disgruntled with Mr. Perry. It must have long been obvious to both men that if Parke's will had not been admitted to probate a far simpler and juster division of his property would have taken place. He wrote Byrd:

> You tell me Mr. Perry informs you that he had a smart letter from me; about the charges of Col. Parks tryall. I shall, and will stand by what I have writ; and can never think I ought to

pay one penny; for a thing that in the main did me and you to such an injury that Mr. Perry can never repair. Had that will not been proved; I need not say what would have bin the consequence. Besides Mr. Perry Senior had my positive order to the contrary.[17]

When, in 1725, a demand arrived from an unexpected quarter, Custis again wrote Byrd:

This comes to inform you that one who calls himself Dunbar Parke, haveing married that little bastard of Col. Parkes in Antigua, has writt me a very smart letter a copy of which I have sent to Mr. Perry; and demands £10,000 of me, it being debts of Col. Parke recovered by law in Antigua.[18]

Thus began a new and prolonged phase of attempted procurement by Parke's heirs in the Islands. Lucy Chester Parke had indeed lived to grow up; and her half-brother, Captain Julius Caesar, mindful of the overall terms of the will, had kept in touch with her. She had married Thomas Dunbar Parke (both of them had been entirely obedient to the required change of name) and by 1736 was his widow. As his brother's executor, Charles Dunbar, surveyor general of the Leewards, spent a good part of the next twenty-one years in an effort to prove that the intent of Parke's will was to charge all his debts, including those in Antigua, to the English and American estate. He sued the Custises repeatedly; at one point he filed a lengthy petition with Governor Gooch.

In 1736, Byrd attempted to weaken the Dunbar case by appealing to Julius Caesar; in an exceptionally friendly letter he proposed that if Julius

Coud prevail with Mrs. Dunbar to side against her righteous brother Charles, it woud do knights service. She may certainly release the debt if she pleases. . . . It will make the suit appear much more monstrous & unnatural, to have one of Col. Parkes murderers claim in his own right any part of his estate.[19]

The ploy did not work, and the appellant did not give up. Not until the reign of George II, in the forty-seventh year after Parke's murder, was the last presentation of the Dunbar suit (of which the appellant's case still survives) scheduled "To be heard before the Right Honourable the Lords of the Committee of his Majesty's most Honourable Privy Council, for Plantation Affairs, at the Council Chamber at *Whitehall*, on Friday, the 24 Day of June, 1757."[20]

At about the time that Byrd wrote to Julius Caesar in 1736, the pressure for ready money that had been upon him for these many years became acute. He had just finished doing over his house, Westover; and while much of the cost could be met in kind with materials from his own land, some of it had to be paid for in money. His need was so great that he put the house up for sale, but was so far without a potential buyer. Of course, he did not really want to sell, but the same letter in which he asks Julius Caesar for help with Mrs. Dunbar indicates that his godson had been attempting to find a purchaser for him: "Hearing no farther from your friend Mr. Freeman about Westover, I have offered it to my old acquaintance Mr. Peter Beckford of Jamaica, and expect his answer. I must dispose thereof to make myself easy, & emancipate my self from the slavery to which all debtors are subject."[21] (Because of that slavery, in January 1740 Byrd confided to his diary, wistfully and even jealously, his inability to match the grandeur with which the colony's current secretary, John Carter, was dressing and entertaining at Shirley, only a few miles upriver.)

Yet in spite of the Dunbar harassment, Parke's heirs in Virginia also received evidence that the inhabitants of Antigua included a third group, beyond the rioting looters and the legatees in search of endowment of whose presence they were already fully and painfully aware. There were also some devoted friends. Because of them, the likeness of his Queen that was in the locket Her Majesty gave Parke after Blenheim is in the possession of his American descendants today. The farrier—or was it the butcher?—who snatched it from Parke's uniform when the rioters stripped him, appears to have

Miniature of Queen Anne from Parke's locket. The Queen gave Parke this portrait by an unknown artist for bringing her the news of Blenheim. Stolen during or after the riot at the time of Parke's murder, it was later recovered, without its frame, and returned to his family in Virginia.—*Reproduced courtesy of its present owner, Mrs. van S. Merle-Smith*

been less interested in the miniature than in the diamond-encrusted solid gold frame containing it. Somewhere along the way, the frame disappeared. Today's frame is plain gold and modern, but the Queen is still there. No available word states by whom, or even when, its recovery and return was managed, but the miniature continues to descend in its intended ownership, in the United States.

That line of descent gives Parke an unmatched status as a family member of American heroes. Fanny's son, Daniel Parke Custis, married Martha Dandridge, subsequently the wife of George Washington. Daniel and Martha's children, Jackie and Patsy, were the familiars of Mount Vernon; and George Washington Parke Custis, Jackie's son by Eleanor Calvert of the Baltimore family, became the adopted son of the first president of the United States after his

The Washington Family. In 1798, the American artist Edward Savage (1761–1817) published this copperplate based on his earlier oil painting. One of the most popular engravings of the time, it brought Savage some $10,000 in its first year. The Mount Vernon family is gathered round a table; across from the first president of the United States are his wife, her two grandchildren, and their servant, Billy Lee. The older boy, George Washington Parke Custis, who stands close to Washington, his adopted father, is the great-great-grandson of Daniel Parke II.—*Reproduced courtesy of the Mount Vernon Ladies Association*

own father died an early death of fever caught at Yorktown during Washington's victory over Cornwallis in 1781.

Soon after the turn of the century, the Custises became the Washingtons' close neighbors. George Washington Parke Custis inherited from his own father some 1,100 acres of land overlooking the new capital of the new country. In July 1804, he married Mary Lee Fitz-hugh, daughter of William Fitzhugh, formerly of Chatham near Fredericksburg and latterly a resident of Alexandria, and built the beautiful Greek Revival house that still commands its view of the city of Washington. He named it Arlington after the family plantation on the Eastern Shore.

The marriage of their daughter, Mary Ann Randolph Custis, celebrated there in 1831, was one of the great Virginia weddings of the period. The bridegroom was the handsome young West Pointer, Lt. Robert E. Lee, son of Light Horse Harry, Revolutionary War general and three-time governor of Virginia. Born at Stratford, he had lived during his boyhood in Alexandria. The new Arlington was the couple's home for thirty years, until after Colonel Lee became commander-in-chief of the army of the Confederacy.

As soon as the Civil War was over, the Lee family's connection with George Washington was renewed in a civilian setting. Back in 1796, after a thoughtful choice among possible locations and institutions, Washington had presented a major endowment to the educational institution previously known as Liberty Hall, at Lexington, Virginia. The name was then changed to Washington College. It was to Washington College in Lexington that the Lees moved in 1865 when Lee accepted the presidency of the college known today as Washington and Lee University.

Even though these relationships did not bear the Parke family name, the Parkes, father and son, would have found recognition and taken pride in the presence of their blood, in later years, at the heart of American history.

Endnotes

Chapter 1

1. H. R. McIlwaine, ed., *The Journals of the House of Burgesses of Va.* (Richmond: Va. State Library, 1903), p. 173. [Hereafter referred to as *Journals, Va. Burgesses.*]

2. For an account of the early excavations, see Samuel H. Yonge, *The Site of Old "James Towne"* (Richmond: Heritage Press, 1907). The Historic American Buildings Survey, a cooperative venture under the National Park Service, is currently engaged in an assessment of subsequent work.

3. Cited as preserved among family papers at Wotton, by Gideon D. Scull, *The Evelyns in America*, reprint of private ed. (Oxford: Parker & Co., 1881), pp. 531–32.

4. James City County, Patent Book 3, Aug. 2, 1652, p. 144. On May 19, 1655, p. 334, the same tract was transferred to Christopher Knipe.

Chapter 2

1. Eric Smith, *Insights into a Thousand Years of Parish History* (Long Ditton: Rector and Churchwardens of St. Mary's Church, 1980).

2. John Aubrey, *The Natural History and Antiquities of the County of Surrey* (London: E. Curll, 1719), pp. 244–45.

3. The Parochial Church Council, *St. John's Church, Wotton, Surrey*, 1978.

4. E. S. de Beer, ed., John Evelyn, *Diary* (Oxford: Clarendon Press, 1955) Feb. 26, 1649, vol. II, p. 551. [Hereafter referred to as Evelyn, *Diary.*]

5. Ibid, May 26, 1671, vol. III, pp. 577–79.

Chapter 3

1. Elizabeth Doonan, "Eighteenth Century English Merchants," *Journal of Economic and Business History*, 4 (1931): 1, 1–98.

2. British Library, London, MS Collection, Add. MS 14831 [Hereafter referred to as Brit. Lib.]

3. William Purdie Thelvar, *A Londoner's Diary of 1906–07*, to which is added a *Diary of Micajah Perry, Lord Mayor 1738–39* (London, 1920), passim.

4. William Fitzhugh to Nicholas Hayward, Dec. 19, 1693, *Virginia Magazine of History and Biography* 4 (1896–97):180–81. [Hereafter *Va. Mag.*]

Chapter 4

1. J. A. C. Chandler and T. B. Thomas, *Colonial Virginia* (Richmond: Times Dispatch Publishing Co., 1901), p. 254.
2. Project of Colonial Williamsburg Foundation, *York County, Va., Records, Deeds, Orders & Wills*, Series 3, p. 183. [Hereafter referred to as *DOW*, (series), p.]
3. *DOW* (4) 237.
4. Ibid. (3) 4.
5. Ibid. (3) 135.
6. Ibid.
7. Ibid. (3) 169.
8. Ibid. (3) 168.
9. Ibid. (3) 118.
10. Ibid. (3) 111.
11. *Journals, Va. Burgesses*, vol. I, p. 173.
12. Louis B. Wright, *First Gentlemen of Virginia* (San Marino, Calif.: The Huntington Library, 1940), pp. 330–31.
13. The will of Daniel Parke, Sr., proved 16 Sept. 1679, is reproduced in *Va. Mag.* 14 (1907):174.
14. Though not free from inaccuracies, much information about Daniel Parke, Jr., is contained in Ruth May Bourne, "John Evelyn the Diarist and his Cousin, Daniel Parke II," *Va. Mag.* 78 (1970):3–33; Edward W. Greenfield, "Some New Aspects of the Life of Daniel Parke," ibid. 54 (1946):306–15, includes in full Jane Parke's letter of resignation.

Chapter 5

1. *DOW* (3) 25.
2. Charles Campbell, *History of the Colony and Ancient Dominion of Virginia* (Spartanburg, S.C.: The Reprint Co., 1965), pp. 327–28.
3. William Edwin Hemphill, Marvin Wilson Schegel, and Sadie Ethel Engelberg, *Cavalier Commonwealth* (New York: McGraw Hill, 1957), p. 84.
4. *Dyrham Park, Gloucestershire*, The National Trust, 1985; Gertrude Ann Jacobsen, *William Blathwayt* (New Haven: Yale University Press); and Humphrey Milford (Oxford: Oxford University Press) 1932, passim.

Chapter 6

1. Evelyn, *Diary*, Feb. 23, 1690, vol. V, pp. 6–7.

2. Evelyn MS, Christ Church College MS Collection, Oxford, Unbound MS No. 39, July 13, 1692.

3. *DOW* (8) 23.

4. Ibid., 239.

5. Ibid., 340–42.

6. Public Record Office, Calendar of State Papers, America & West Indies, Jan. 1693–May 14, 1696, March 29, 1693, no. 227, p. 69. [Hereafter referred to as PRO CSP, Am. & W.I., vol. date, date of item, no., p.]

7. Ibid., Oct. 23, 1693, no. 638, p. 190.

8. Evelyn MS, Christ Church College, Original Letter E no. 656, p. 585.

9. Ibid., Original Letter E no. 657, p. 702.

10. Ibid., Unbound Letters, April 4, 1694.

11. Ibid., Letter Book Epistolarum Liber Quartus, 1679–99, p. 174.

12. William Stevens Perry, ed., *Historical Collections Relating to the American Colonial Church*, 5 vols. (New York: AMS Press, 1969), vol. I, *Virginia*, pp. 69–71. [Hereafter Perry, *Historical Collections*.]

13. Rutherford Goodwin, *A Brief and True Report Concerning Williamsburg in Virginia*, 3rd ed. (Richmond: Dietz, 1941), p. 22.

14. "A Memorial," concerning Sir Edmund Andros, Governor of Virginia, by Dr. Blair, 1697, in Perry, *Historical Collections*, vol. I, p. 23.

15. PRO CSP, Colonial Papers, vol. 14, Jan. 1693–May 14, 1696, June 4, 1695, no. 1870, p. 496.

16. W. A. R. Goodwin, *A Historical Sketch of Bruton Parish Church* (Petersburg, Va.: Franklin Press Co., 1903), p. 20.

17. Perry, *Historical Collections*, "Blair Memorial," 1697, pp. 24–28.

18. Ibid., pp. 54–57.

19. Ibid., p. 48.

20. Ibid., p. 28.

21. Executive Journals, Council of Colonial Virginia, vol. I, June 11, 1680–June 22, 1699, March 1, 1696, p. 362.

22. Ibid., April 23, 1697.

23. *DOW* (11) 243.

Chapter 7

1. Robert Mudie, *Hampshire, Its past and present condition, and future prospects* (London, 1838), p. 284.

2. Evelyn, *Diary*, March 1–5, 1671, vol. III, p. 573.

3. George Washington Parke Custis, *Recollections and Private Memoirs of Washington,* by his adopted son, George Washington Parke Custis, with a memoir of the author by his daughter; and illustrative and explanatory notes by Benjamin Lossing (New York: Derby & Jackson, 1860), p. 15. [Hereafter referred to as Custis, *Memoirs of Washington.*]

4. *A letter to a Minister of State concerning the Pretended Prince of Wales being proclaimed of England in France,* printed for A. Bell at the Cros-Keys and Bible in Cornhill; and B. Lintot at the *Middle-Temple* Gate in Fleet Street (London, 1701), p. 21.

5. William Stebbins, *Peterborough,* (London: MacMillan, 1890), p. 11.

6. Maj. Gen. Sir Richard Luce, *The History of the Abbey and Town of Malmesbury* (Malmsbury: Friends of Malmesbury Abbey, 1979), p. 162.

7. Halifax to Wharton, 21 December 1700, in A. L. Browne, *Lord Halifax and the Malmesbury Election in 1701,* transcribed in the *Wiltshire Archaeological & Natural History Magazine,* vol. XLVII, nos. 162–66, (June 1935–June 1937), p. 503.

8. PRO CSP Domestic, Charles II, 266, Oct. 20, 1669, no. 152, pp. 541–42.

9. *House of Commons Journals,* Jan. 16, 1701, vol. 13, p. 682.

10. Ibid., Jan. 29, 1701, pp. 711–12. All discussion of the Parke case and Peterborough occurs on these pages.

11. Parliamentary Diary of Sir Richard Corks, Bodleian Library, Oxford, Bod. MS b 210, f. lv.

12. *House of Commons Journals,* vol. 13, Feb. 26, 1701, p. 766.

13. Custis, *Memoirs of Washington,* pp. 23–24.

Chapter 8

1. Among the many sources covering Marlborough's preparation for the 1704 campaign, two deserve special attention: George Macauley Trevelyan, *Blenheim* (London: Longmans, Green, 1935); and Winston Churchill, *Marlborough, His Life and Times* (New York: Scribner's, 1935).

2. Evelyn, *Diary*, Dec. 20, 1702, pp. 524–26.

Chapter 9

1. English Army Lists and Commissioner Reports, vol. IV, pp. 195, 228, 265, 278.

2. The Blenheim Bounty of March 1705, Part II, p. 2.

3. Brit. Lib., Add. MS 4741, f. 1.

4. Ibid., Add. MS 4741, f. 2.

5. PRO CSP, Domestic, 1703–1704, p. 336.

6. *Select Passages from the Diary and Letters of the late John Blackader, Esq.*, formerly lieutenant colonel of the XXVI or Cameronian Regiment of Foot, and afterwards Deputy Governor of Stirling Castle, with a preface by John Newton (Edinburgh: Ritchie, 1806), p. 14.

7. Ibid., p. 16.

Chapter 10

1. Brit. Lib., Add. MS 4741, ff. 5–5v.

2. Ibid.

3. Ibid.

Chapter 11

1. Louis de Vouvroy, Duc de Saint-Simon, *Historical Memoirs*, Lucy Norton, ed. and trans. (New York: McGraw-Hill, 1967), pp. 251–52.

2. Unnamed French aide-de-camp's description of the battle of Blenheim, captured, translated and published in a bilingual edition (London: John Nutt, 1704), p. 9.

3. Marlborough to Sarah, Aug. 13, 1704, in William Coxe, *Memoirs of Marlborough*, 3 vols., revised by John Wade, new ed. (London: George Bell & Sons, 1896, 1905, 1907), vol. I, p. 231. [Hereafter referred to as Coxe, *Memoirs of Marlborough*.] After surviving various vicissitudes, this note today is exhibited at Blenheim Palace.

Chapter 12

1. Brit. Lib., Add. MS (St) 7069, f. 171.

2. Ibid., f. 172.

3. Ibid., Add. MS (St) 7066, f. 15.

4. Queen to Sarah, Aug. 21, 1704, in Coxe, *Memoirs of Marlborough*, vol. I, p. 231.

5. PRO London, Venetian Transcripts 46, PRO 31/14/46, XCO364.

6. Brit. Lib., Add. MS 17677 ZZ, f. 380.

7. *The Observator*, vol. III, no. 41.

8. A. Stratford to Thomas Coke, M. P. at Melbourne. H. M. Stationery Office, 1889. August 10, 1704. Historical MSS Commission, 12th Report, Appendix, Part III, 1889, p. 39; in the MS of the earl Cowper, K.G., Melbourne Hall, Derbyshire.

9. Evelyn, *Diary*, Aug. 13, 1704, vol. V, p. 578.

10. Henry L. Snyder, ed., *Marlborough-Godolphin Correspondence* (Oxford: Clarendon Press, 1975); vol. I, no. 371, p. 361.

11. Narcissus Luttrell, *A Brief Historical Relation of State Affairs from September 1678 to April 1714* (Oxford: Oxford University Press, 1957) vol. V, p. 457. [Hereafter referred to as Luttrell, *Historical Relation*.]

12. John Hill Burton, *A History of the Reign of Queen Anne* (Edinburgh and London: Wm. Blackwood & Sons, 1830), vol. I, p. 305.

13. Evelyn, *Diary*, Sept. 7, 1704, vol. V, p. 578.

14. Calendar of Virginia State Papers, Dec. 15, 1704, pp. 86–87.

Chapter 13

1. James Blair to Philip Ludwell, Jan. 6, 1704/5. 3 (*William & Mary*) series (1) p. 17.

2. Perry, *Historical Collections*, vol. I, pp. 179–81.

3. Luttrell, *Brief Relation*, vol. V, pp. 458, 528.

4. Leonidas Dodson, *Alexander Spotswood* (Philadelphia: University of Pennsylvania Press), and Humphrey Milford (Oxford: Oxford University Press, 1932), appendix I, pp. 304–305.

5. Brit. Lib., Add. MS 61364, f. 60.

6. *Journals of the House of Commons*, vol. 15, Oct. 25, 1707–April 1, 1708, Nov. 13, 1705, p. 22.

7. Luttrell, *Brief Relation*, vol. V, p. 611.

8. Jane Parke to Daniel Parke, July 12, 1705, Virginia Historical Society Collection, Custis Family Papers, MSS 1, C9698 a 1–2, Custis Section 1.

Chapter 14

1. Marion Tinling, ed., *Correspondence of the Three William Byrds of Westover, Virginia 1684–1706*, published for the Virginia Historical Society (Charlottesville: University of Virginia Press, 1977), vol. I, pp. 256, 258, 252, 258. [Hereafter VHS]

2. Custis, *Memoirs of Washington*, p. 16.

3. Maude H. Woodfin, ed., translated and collated by Marion Tinling, Egmont MSS in the custody of S. C. Radcliffe, HMC, PRO, cited in *Another Secret Diary of William Byrd of Westover, 1739–1741* (Richmond: Dietz Press, 1942), p. xx.

4. Custis, *Memoirs of Washington*, p. 24.

5. Micajah Perry to John Custis, VHS, MS 2, 4298 a.

6. Philip Ludwell II to Philip Ludwell III, VHS, MSS 1, L51, f5.

7. Ibid.

8. Ibid.

9. Philip Ludwell III to Philip Ludwell II, VHS, MSS 1, C9698 a 6–21.

10. Louis Wright and Marion Tinling, eds., *The Secret Diary of William Byrd of Westover, 1709–12* (Richmond: Dietz Press, 1941), p. 102.

11. A copy of the inventory made at the time of Parke's death is in the collections of the VHS.

12. Byrd, *Secret Diary*, p. 48.

13. Ibid., pp. 296–97, 494.

14. Byrd, *Correspondence*, vol. I, pp. 305–306.

15. E. T. Crowson, "John Custis of Arlington," in *Virginia Cavalcade*, Virginia State Library, Richmond, vol. 20 (Summer 1970): 17.

16. Byrd, *Correspondence*, vol. I, pp. 347, 351.

Chapter 15

1. Louis B. Wright, ed., Richard Eburne, *A Plain Pathway to Plantations*, 1624, published for the Folger Shakespeare Library (Ithaca, N.Y.: Cornell University Press, 1962), p. 3.

2. Richard S. Dunn, *Sugar and Slaves* (Chapel Hill: University of North Carolina Press, 1972), p. 143.

3. Hugh Edward Egerton, *A Short History of British Colonial Policy*, 11th ed. revised by A. P. Newton (London: Methuen, 1945), p. 144.

4. Lothrop Withington, "Virginia Gleanings in England," in *Va. Mag.*, vol. 20, pp. 372–81.

5. PRO CSP, Am. & W.I., vol. 23, 1706–June 1708, Aug. 4, 1707, no. 1077, p. 519.

6. Ibid., Aug. 28, 1706, no. 473, p. 199.

7. Codrington to Orrery, Sept. 19, 1706, Codrington MSS Collection, Codrington Park, Gloucestershire, MS B, f. 19.

8. PRO CSP, Am. & W.I., vol. 23, 1706–June 1708, Jan. 19, 1707, no. 723, p. 358.

9. Ibid., Jan. 13, 1707, no. 717, p. 356.

10. Ibid., March 28, 1707, no. 834, p. 411.

11. Ibid., Aug. 4, 1707, no. 1077, p. 579; Marlborough-Godolphin Correspondence, vol. II, no. 810, June 5, 1707.

12. Brit. Lib., Add. MS 61643.

13. Ibid., Add. MS 61641A.

14. PRO CSP, Am. & W.I., vol. 23, Oct. 31, 1706, no. 560, p. 286.

15. Ibid., March 6, 1708, no. 1380, p. 690.

16. Ibid., June 16, no. 1579, p. 751.

17. Colonel Parke to the Duke of Marlborough, 1709, Historical MSS Commission, 15th Report, Appendix, Pt. II, the MSS of J. Eliot Hodgkin, Esq., F.R.A., of Richmond, Surrey, London, H. M. Stationery Office, 1897, p. 345.

18. Brit. Lib., Add. MSS 61637, ff. 90–93v.

19. Byrd, *Secret Diary*, pp. 16, 18, 80, 94.

20. PRO, CSP, Am. & W.I., vol. 24, June 1708–1709, Sept. 20, 1709, no. 741, pp. 469–71.

Chapter 16

[Note: Volumes 25 and 26 of the PRO's Colonial State Papers, America and West Indies, assemble the main source material on Parke's murder, including not only the official reports sent to London, but the conflicting affidavits collected soon after the event. Additional items are the rival pamphlets privately produced by various factions of the settlers, some defending the colonists as aggrieved upholders of the rights of Englishmen, others representing supporters of the governor as the defender of imperial order. The earliest of these ephemeral and anonymously distributed broadsides appeared in 1713: "Some Instances of the Oppression and Male Administration of Col. Parke"; the last, "The History of Col. Parke's Administration . . . whilst he was Captain General and Chief Governour of the Leeward Islands," came out in 1717 and was known to have been written by George French, a close friend of the governor. Copies of one or more of these fugitive works are to be found in the collections of the Library of Congress in Washington and the Virginia Historical Society in Richmond.]

1. Byrd, *Secret Diary*, June 10, 1710, pp. 189–90, and Aug. 15, p. 218.

2. PRO CSP Am. & W.I., vol. 25, 1710–June 1711, Sept. 9, 1710, no. 391, pp. 180–214; and no. 390, pp. 187–89.

3. Ibid., vol. 26, no. 484, p. 256.

4. Anon., "Some Instances of the Oppression and Male Administration of Col. PARKE, late Governor of the Leeward Islands" (London, 1713), p. 1.

5. PRO CSP Am. & W.I., vol. 25, no. 674 iv (b), pp. 394–95.

6. Ibid., vol. 25, nos. 674–78, Feb. 23, 1711, nos. 674–77; and Feb. 27, 1711, 386–401.

7. Brit. Lib. Add. MS 61293.

Chapter 17

1. Coxe, *Memoirs of Marlborough*, vol. III, p. 124.

2. *Memoirs of the Life of James*, late Duke of Ormonde, extracted from his own private memoirs, lately printed at the Hague, in French; and now first translated into English (London: Stanton, 1738), p. 239.

3. PRO CSP, Am. & W.I., vol. 25, 1710–June 1711, April 14, 1711, no. 809, pp. 459–461.

4. Ibid., vol. 26, July 1711–June 28, 1712, May 2, 1712, no. 396, p. 274.

5. Byrd, *Secret Diary*, p. 328.

6. Ibid., p. 585.

7. Byrd, *Correspondence*, vol. I, p. 280.

8. Ibid., p. 281.

9. Ibid.

10. Ibid., p. 284.

11. Ibid., p. 285.

12. Byrd, *Secret Diary*, p. 517.

13. Ibid., p. 518.

14. Ibid., p. 520.

15. Byrd, *Correspondence*, vol. I, p. 287.

16. Ibid., p. 323.

17. Ibid., p. 351.

18. Ibid., pp. 351–52.

19. Ibid., vol. II, p. 472.

20. VHS Collection, Rare, K110 D82, photo, oversize.

21. Byrd, *Correspondence*, vol. II, p. 473.

Index